ROMAN CATHOLIC WRITINGS ON DOCTRINAL DEVELOPMENT BY JOHN HENRY NEWMAN

Roman Catholic Writings on Doctrinal Development by John Henry Newman

*Edited, with Translation and Commentary
by James Gaffney*

Sheed & Ward
Kansas City

On the cover:

Bust of John Henry Newman was made circa 1880 in London by M. Racci and is located at the University of Notre Dame. Photo by Steve Moriarity.

Sheed & Ward™ is a service of The National Catholic Reporter Publishing Company.

Library of Congress Cataloguing-in-Publication Data
Newman, John Henry, 1801-1890.
  [Selections. English. 1997]
    Roman Catholic writings on doctrinal development /
by John Henry Newman ; edited, with translation and
commentary by James Gaffney.
      p.   cm.
   ISBN: 1-55612-973-4 (alk. paper)
   1. Dogma, Development of. 2. Catholic Church—Doctrines
—History. I. Gaffney, James.
  BX4705.N5A25 1997
  230'.2—dc21   97-16289
                                                  CIP

Published by: Sheed & Ward
                  115 E. Armour Blvd.
                  P.O. Box 419492
                  Kansas City, MO 64141-6492

To order, call: (800) 333-7373

Cover design by Jane Pitz.

www.natcath.com/sheedward

Contents

Preface

The purpose of the present volume is to make more readily accessible to students of the thought of John Henry Newman two of his writings on a subject that persistently and decisively influenced his religious and intellectual life, namely the preservation and modification of Christian teaching from its apostolic beginnings to its situation in the ecclesiastical diversity and instability of the nineteenth century. How central this matter was to Newman's own spiritual seeking is plain from the fact that his critical – and in many ways – painful decision to forsake the Church of England, in which he was a celebrated leader, for the Church of Rome, in which his presence was always, and often acutely, awkward, was actually made through the very process of writing *An Essay on the Development of Christian Doctrine,* a scholarly treatise that remained uncompleted, broken off abruptly in a climactic ecstasy of prayer and exhortation. This book, incomplete but by no means inconclusive, was published shortly after its author became a Roman Catholic, and immediately submitted for revision to ecclesiastical authorities. Newman's offer to revise was not accepted, on the view that an unaltered version of the work he had composed before becoming a Roman Catholic would be more persuasive to readers. Consequently Newman came into his new church on the strength of an argument which that church had not officially examined or approved. Roman Catholic authorities had, of course, no doubt that Newman had made the right decision. But they had no firm opinion about the rightness of the reasons he had given for making that decision. Indeed most of them had little understanding of those reasons, and little sympathy with the religious perplexities Newman had been trying to resolve. They would have been more than happy to regard Newman's book as the final episode of his ecclesiastically misguided past, and to see him now, as a Roman Catholic, break cleanly with that past and with theological preoccupations he no longer needed to entertain at all. Roman Catholics did not worry about how doctrines had developed. They worried about what doctrines constituted the orthodoxy they were obligated to believe. And they settled such worries by appealing not to history, or even to the Bible, but to the teaching authority of their contemporary church, that is, as they commonly expressed it, to Rome. For many Catholics that was one of the most comforting things about their church.

Conceivably, Newman could have taken this typically Roman Catholic view and let it go at that. He was not half-hearted about the dogmatism of his new church. He believed in the divine authorization of Rome to guarantee revealed truth. He was prepared to revise or even renounce any of his Anglican theological writings, including the very ones that marked his path to Rome. He submitted them unreservedly to official judgment. But no official judgment was delivered, then or ever. Instead, rumors proliferated of unofficial judgments, questioning the usefulness and even the orthodoxy of Newman's views on the development of doctrine. The recent American convert to Roman Catholicism, Orestes Brownson, though an amateur in historical theology, denounced Newman's book as essentially Protestant and unorthodox. It was reported that in Rome itself the book had attracted unfavorable attention from theologians highly regarded by the pope. But such disquieting innuendoes and shadowy adversaries offered Newman no opportunities for candid discussion of even the humblest kind. He felt sure that his views were little understood. He feared they might be very damagingly misunderstood. He hoped to find some way of clarifying them so that the criticism they incurred, even if it remained hostile, would at least be relevant and potentially constructive. There seemed to be no way of accomplishing that goal in England. When it was decided that Newman should be sent to Rome to follow a course of study that would repair the deficiencies of his Anglican priesthood, he saw this as an opportunity to express his ideas with maximum clarity at the very heart of Roman Catholic orthodoxy, and be enlightened by the best qualified of critics. He had no doubt that he had much to learn from Roman Catholic theologians. He was eager to begin learning. And for this, Rome seemed the best of all possible destinations. Even before the journey ended, his disillusionment was already profound.

Newman's journey from England occupied seven weeks, most of them spent in Milan. He was received along the way by French and Italian clergy as a distinguished visitor. He was greatly impressed by the centrality of the Blessed Sacrament in the great Italian churches, by the spontaneous liveliness of popular devotion, and by many signs of continuity with the age of the Fathers of the Church which he especially revered. His encounters with the great orders, especially Dominicans and Jesuits, whom he had expected to admire were disappointing. But most disappointing of all was the intellectual side of Roman Catholicism in Rome itself. Philosophy and theology appeared torpid. The classic authors of Scholastic tradition, with which he had hoped to become familiar, appeared virtually unread. Thoughtful questions presented to his assigned teachers evoked only signs of perplexity. Religious certainty he found everywhere, but in a form that he contrasted with living faith. The profound conservatism and rigid authoritarianism of the ruling Pontiff did not encourage controversy or speculation. It did encourage suspicion of what appeared to be new ideas, and all the more if such ideas seemed to have been imported from outside Roman Catholicism. Newman's association with so dubious a concept as the "development" of Christian doctrine could not, in these circumstances, ingratiate him with his teachers or fellow students. Given the whole-heartedness of his commitment and submission to the Church of Rome it may seem surprising that he did not simply leave the whole matter of doctrinal development behind him, satisfied that his investigations had led him to the church where he belonged, prepared to let his book go out of print and into oblivion, and determined to devote himself henceforth to topics more congenial to Roman Catholic habits of thought. Part of his reason for not doing so was undoubtedly his awareness that the way that had led him from the Church of England to the Church of Rome was a way that other Anglicans might also follow. Indeed his book had ended with an impassioned exhortation for them to do so. If it should now appear that Rome itself viewed that book with distrust or disfavor, his potential contribution to his former correligionists would be stultified. Moreover, Newman was utterly per-suaded that development of doctrine was a matter of enormous theological and religious importance, basic to the scandalous fragmentation of post-Reformation Chris-tianity, and to any realistic hope of eventual reunification. That the Roman Catholic Church took little if any serious interest in this matter could not, for Newman, be a matter of indifference. And it certainly occurred to him that here, if anywhere, he might be able, and indeed obli-gated, to make a distinctive contribution to the Church to which, he had no doubt, God had led him. He did not, therefore, abandon the topic, but looked for new ways of introducing it and entertaining it in harmony with the dispositions and priorities of Roman Catholic culture. His first, and almost pathetically modest effort in this regard, is represented by the first of the two documents contained in this volume, written during his first months in his new church. The other document presented here is a much more audacious one, reflecting some quite new ideas on the subject that took shape late in Newman's life, after much experience, some of it far from pleasant, of Roman Catholicism. But before introducing these documents specifically, it may be useful to some readers to review briefly the place of doctrinal development in Newman's Anglican writings, and to recall some of his other contributions to that subject during his Roman Catholic years. For actual reference, readers may find convenient my edition of most of those writings, with brief commentary, published a few years ago under the title *Conscience, Consensus, and the Development of Doctrine* (New York: Doubleday, 1992).

Why Development of Doctrine Mattered

At risk of belaboring the obvious it is necessary to recall that in Newman's century Christianity presented a spectacle of great ecclesiastical diversity underlain by pervasive mutual recrimination. Viewed from our own era in which ecumenism, irenicism, and indifferentism collectively prevail, and are often difficult to distinguish, it may not be easy to envisage a world, recent though it is, in which ecclesiastical differences were frankly identified as differences between rightness and wrongness, between having preserved and having lost or distorted that saving truth revealed by God in Christ. That truth had been expressed in words by Jesus of Nazareth and entrusted to his Apostles. It had been memorialized in sacred books composed under divine inspiration. It had been proclaimed by missionaries, applied by pastors, explained by

scholars, defended against infidels, upheld against heretics, and defined by authorities empowered by the illumi-
nation of the Holy Spirit. This process of proclamation,
explanation, vindication, and definition generated an
ever-accumulating body of teaching, conceived not as a
heaping up of new information, but as declaration or
elucidation, required by circumstances, of the truth delivered once and for all to the faith of the Apostles. There
were, of course new words, new propositions, new illustrations, new formulations, arguments, and inferences, generated by the varying circumstances of ecclesiastical
history. In that sense there was new doctrine, but only in
that sense; new teaching, but not of new truth or new
revelation. The very purpose of those endless and various
labors of teaching was precisely to see to it that one same
truth could be "believed everywhere, always, and by every-
one," a phrase made famous by the fifth century monk,
Vincent of Lerins, and adopted by Newman as a touch-
stone of doctrinal orthodoxy. For doctrine to develop was
simply for that truth to be imparted, in various ways but
always faithfully and efficaciously, to successive generations of Christians. And the problem with such a conception is, of course, obvious. Suppose there were a true
divine revelation, delivered by Christ and perhaps preserved faultlessly by his Apostles, but suppose that subsequent explanations did not do it justice. Suppose they
fell short of it, or went beyond it, or misconstrued it,
incompetently or even maliciously, and eventually turned
it into something it had not been, something whose alien
features obscured or perverted its original essence. That
this kind of thing could happen was obvious, and that it
had happened repeatedly was a commonplace of Christian history. The very idea that doctrine developed in part
through the refutation of heresy implied that heresy occurred and recurred, and heresy was naturally claimed by
its own adherents to express the original truth.

During Christianity's first centuries the problem here implied found its solution in ecclesiastical authority, trusted by the great body of the faithful to determine which enunciations of doctrine were authentic expressions of the divine revelation, and which were distortions of it. But with the Protestant Reformation that trust in ecclesiastical authority had broken down in much of the Christian world, ushering in a multitude of contending claimants to orthodoxy, and an assortment of opinions as to how those contending claims could be assessed. The most influential of those opinions called for exclusive reliance on the most stable and original witness to Christian truth, the Bible. Yet the Bible itself was subject to a diversity of interpretations, and most of the notorious heresies of the past had made plausible claims to scriptural support. Often enough the conclusive intervention of ecclesiastical authority was precisely concerned with resolving doctrinal disputes predicated on exegetical differences. And whenever that happened the history of doctrine moved into a new phase, with the limits of orthodoxy more fully and clearly expressed in regard to some disputed matter. In that sense, doctrine developed, and had to develop precisely to maintain its authenticity. Quite early in his scholarly career, Newman had studied this process in one of its first and greatest historical occasions, that of the so-called Arian controversy, which had evoked the first great ecumenical council of the church and produced the first great dogmatic definitions of Christian belief. For Newman this was the supreme paradigm of doctrinal development.

Why the Arian Controversy Mattered

John Henry Newman was never a professional scholar in the sense of an unprejudiced explorer of learned questions for their own sake. Scholarship was always for him a means to an end, and the end was always in some sense religious. It began with firm religious premises and pursued religious results. The religious premises were Christian religious premises, and the results were intended to serve Christian purposes. Secular agnosticism was for Newman the most deplorable of human conditions, to which even the opposite excesses of superstition were decidedly preferable. Even defective religion was better than no religion at all, and often a stage on the way to true Christian faith. This notion formed part of Newman's theology of history, which saw, for example, the religious attitudes and philosophies of classical civilization as preparatory for the Christian era and properly contributory to Christian culture. Newman's favorite period in the history of Christianity was the age of the Fathers of the Church, and his favorite Fathers of the Church were those associated with the theological center at Alexandria where neo-Platonic thought was a cherished resource for interpreting Christian revelation. He had a deep personal devotion to the fourth century St. Athanasius of Alexandria, defender of what would ultimately be recognized as Christological orthodoxy against the heretical doctrines referred to collectively as Arianism. There are numerous indications that Newman saw Athanasius as a model for his own vocation, and perceived many aspects of the saint's career as foreshadowing his own. It is not surprising that when Newman accepted an invitation to produce his first major work of scholarship, a history of Church Councils, the book turned out to be something quite different, appropriately entitled *The Arians of the Fourth Century.*

It was the historical context addressed by this work that held Newman's attention to the matter he later referred to as the development of Christian doctrine. For it was here, in the century of controversy that evoked the first two general Councils of the Church and their dogmatic definitions which became part of the Christian profession of faith, that doctrine "developed" momentously and conspicuously, as a precedent for all subsequent developments. For the heart of the Arian controversy was the question of Christ's divinity, inevitably linked to the question of his humanity and the relation of the one to the other. The credal affirmations that emerged, that Christ is fully and unequivocally divine, that he is also fully and unequivocally human, are beliefs that, in the view of their defenders, were held from the apostolic age and attested by the inspired scriptures. But the process of argument that led to these affirmations required that something be said by way of explanation to those who raised objections. If Christ was fully divine, yet referred to God as his Father, how is monotheism to be sustained? And if he was also fully human, how can man and God, creature and Creator, be said, in any literal sense, to be one? Modern Christians are familiar with the devices of religious metaphysics, adapted from classical philosophy, that, used to answer these questions, became themselves features of dogma. Christ the Son shared with his Father one nature or substance; he was, in a Latin term, *consubstantialis,* or in Greek, *homoousios.* And his divine nature was united with his human nature in a single person, *persona, hypostasis.* Whatever may be thought of the adequacy of these explanations, and their fidelity to the actual beliefs of the first Christians, they were certainly terminological novelties, representing notions previously unfamiliar to ordinary Christian usage. In that sense, for them to have become explicit elements of Christian doctrine is clear enough evidence that, in some sense, Christian doctrine "developed;" it exhibited features at a later stage that were not previously apparent. But the point of calling such features developments is to emphasize that they are not strictly adventitious, new

items brought in and tacked on. In calling them developments it is implied that, despite their apparent newness,
they were in another and deeper sense, inherent in the
original completed revelation of Christ to his apostles.

Thus Newman's study of the Church of the Fathers,
the period of church history in which Christianity took
on its basic doctrinal shape, illustrated the inevitability of
doctrinal development. Questions must arise and controversies develop that gave rise to new formulations of belief
designed precisely to preserve and elucidate its original
import. Christological and Trinitarian doctrines were
simply the answers given to questions about revealed
truth that had not yet been raised in the age of the
apostles. The answers had been implicit from the start,
and if the questions could have been put intelligibly to
the Apostles themselves they would have given equivalent
answers. In the definitive settling of the Arian question
Christianity had not acquired new revelation but, under
the guidance of the Spirit, new understanding and new
formulations to express and preserve it. Newman sadly
recognized that such developments were typically precipi-
tated by crises of misunderstanding, like that of the Arian
heretics, and that doctrinal developments arose out of
painful events. In an idyllically tranquil, faultlessly believing community of Christians, developments might find no
occasion, and dogmatic definitions be superfluous. But
that was not reality, and developments were responses to
reality.

Underdevelopment, Overdevelopment, and a Via Media

Given Newman's normative appreciation of the church of
the Fathers, what he spontaneously looked for in the
ecclesiastical chaos of his own day was that church's rec-
ognizably legitimate heir. Where, if anywhere, in the

Victorian age, would a St. Athanasius find himself at home? Not, certainly, in any church that excluded developments, condemned non-biblical formulations of doctrine, despaired of the church's teaching authority, and offered no better guarantor of truth than private judgment by individual Christians. Such was Newman's understanding of what he called Protestantism, and nothing seemed to him more obvious than that Protestantism was not the church of the Fathers. Turning away from Protestantism, what Newman perceived to be the opposite extremity was Roman Catholicism. Here there might seem to be no scarcity of doctrinal developments, no misgivings about authority, nor any naiveté about the practical sufficiency of Scripture and private judgment. Newman did in fact considered the Church of Rome to be, in principle, on the right track. But only in principle, and not in practice. Newman argued, as Roman Catholics did, that to cling to Scripture while rejecting Tradition was an untenable position, if only because the very conviction that Scripture was the inspired word of God was one that depended on Tradition; Scripture did not guarantee itself. He meant by Tradition, broadly speaking, what Christians had always, at least implicitly, believed. The trouble with the Roman Catholic Church was that its doctrines appeared to go far beyond the defensible limits of Tradition, including some that Christians had by no means always believed, and that did not enjoy the support of the Church of the Fathers. As Newman put it, the test that was failed by the Church of Rome was the test of Antiquity. That left Newman pursuing an ideal position in between the doctrinal underdevelopment of Protestantism, and the doctrinal overdevelopment of Roman Catholicism. He hoped the Church of England might be the realization of that ideal middle path between two opposite kinds of error, and argued in defense of that hope in a work appropriately entitled *The Via Media of the Anglican Church,* whose two volumes contain Newman's most elaborate criticism of the doctrinal position of the Roman Catholic Church, as well as his strongest defense of the Anglican position. Since it would would be only eight years before Newman left the Church of England for the Church of Rome, he had during that time to accomplish a twofold labor of self-refutation He had to persuade himself that his hope of demonstrating an Anglican *Via Media* was unrealistic. He had also to persuade himself that the Church of Rome did not after all fail the test of Antiquity. The first of these tasks was the easier. The Church of England in which he lived seemed to Newman to be moving in a direction that was unmistakably Protestant. The *Via Media* was, he sadly concluded, only a theory, and a theory whose departure from the facts had become flagrant. Given the structure of Newman's original argument, his only hope lay in a reinterpretation of Roman Catholic doctrine, and especially of those doctrinal features that seemed neither scriptural nor, in any acceptable sense, traditional. To accomplish that reinterpretation, the notion of doctrinal development was absolutely crucial.

A Theory of Development

Newman's reflections on the development of doctrine, first stimulated by his study of the Arian controversy and later more personally and religiously motivated by the collapse of his *Via Media* theory, became the basis of a new theory, first expounded only two years before his conversion to the Roman Catholic Church. It was presented as the last of his *Fifteen Sermons Preached Before the University of Oxford,* a series of religious lectures delivered at St. Mary's, Oxford, on the general subject of faith and reason.

The final sermon was entitled "The Theory of Developments in Religious Doctrine" and suggestively introduced by the Gospel passage, "Mary kept all these things, pondering them in her heart." The passage is understood to present Mary as the ideal Christian believer who not only receives revealed truth, but thinks about it and thinks with it, and in the process, inevitably, develops it. Mary's faith represents not only that of simple, unlearned Christians, but that "of the doctors of the Church also, who have to investigate and weigh and define as well as to profess the Gospel; to draw the line between truth and heresy; to anticipate or remedy the various aberrations of wrong reason; to combat pride or recklessness with their own arms; and thus to triumph over the sophist and the innovator." This is an excellent summary of how Newman perceived doctrinal development, and the sermon is an admirable description of how it takes place. Essentially it is a process of gradually unfolding implications, progressively realizing the potentialities of understanding that deliberation and argument bring to consciousness. Newman's subtle and persuasive account of how fundamental ideas seem to expand, deepen, and ramify under intellectual scrutiny is an impressive contribution to the intellectual side of the psychology of religion. In the light of this analysis of the normal way in which profound ideas gradually disclose their fuller significance, Newman proposed that for Christian doctrine not to develop would be the incredible thing, whereas the evidence of its having developed merely attests its vitality.

It was less than three years after his famous sermon on development that Newman completed, or rather concluded his famous book on that subject which reflected the final steps of his historical and theological transition from Anglicanism to Roman Catholicism. Here Newman considers not only the normality of development and the broad characteristics of its psychology, but the harder problem of how to ascertain that supposed developments from an original truth are not really distortions of it. For if it is obvious that ideas develop, it might seem equally obvious that their developments are not always harmonious, often becoming the competing tenets of rival schools of thought, each claiming to be the sole legitimate heir of an original body or system of beliefs. And nowhere is this more apparent than among Christianity's rival claimants to orthodoxy. A distinction must therefore be made between faithful developments and unfaithful ones. Newman reserves the term development for the former, referring to the latter as corruptions, that is, alien, malignant growths. As already noted, Newman in the *Via Media* found Roman Catholicism rich in developments, but he had found it hardly less abounding in corruptions.

In his *Essay on the Development of Christian Doctrine*, Newman adopts a much more systematic approach. The first part of the book deals with development in general, distinguishing different modes of development, and considering what kinds of ideas do tend to develop and what kinds do not. The argument is illustrated both from secular history and from Christian doctrine. Material from the earlier sermon on development is repeated and elaborated. In citing the *Via Media*, Newman's abandonment of that thesis leads him to refer to it merely as the work of "a certain writer" as though his later opinions had severed him from his earlier self. The second part of the book is also systematically organized, constituting almost a methodology. Here Newman offers a set of definite criteria for distinguishing true developments from corruptions of doctrine. These comprise seven "notes" of genuine development. The final seven chapters of the book deal with each in turn, applying them to appropriate doctrines, including most of those for which Roman Catholicism has been most severely criticized by Protestants. Much of this part of the book reads like an undisguised

Roman Catholic apologia and the reader is unlikely to be surprised when it concludes in the words of an impassioned convert, bidding others to follow where he had been led. Newman himself must have been acutely surprised that his "Roman" reinterpretation of development was viewed with great suspicion in Rome itself.

The two documents presented in the following pages represent Newman's first and last attempts as a Roman Catholic to share his reflections on doctrinal development with his fellow Catholics. They are very different kinds of documents, reflecting very different periods of Newman's life as a Roman Catholic.

A Note on The Translation

Translating into English the Latin work of an English writer raises certain problems. The problems are increased if the translation is undertaken long after the original was composed. And there is an additional difficulty if the original writer was a distinguished English stylist. Newman's elegant prose style is well known and justly celebrated. His Latin style was much more pedestrian and, in the present work it is not improved by a mixing of classical and medieval Scholastic usages. Moreover, one who is familiar with Newman's English will often have little doubt of how he would have expressed in English what he has written in Latin. Nevertheless, it seems intolerably artificial for a translator at the end of the twentieth century to translate Newman's Latin into a simulation of his mid-Victorian English style. I have sought a compromise by translating into an English which, though modern and not Newman's, is not jarringly unlike the way he typically expressed himself.

In the original manuscript, Newman left wide right-hand margins in which Perrone wrote his comments.

Sometimes, however, Newman's text flows over into that space. In the present version, Perrone's comments are identified by numbers in Newman's text, and then given in sequence on separate pages after each section, like endnotes.

On the Development of Catholic Dogma

(De Catholici Dogmatis Evolutione)

Introduction

As discussed in the preface, Newman's initiatory experiences as a convert to Roman Catholicism were in many ways awkward and in some respects acutely distressing. Much of the awkwardness arose from his being treated as a neophyte aspirant to the Roman Catholic clergy while recognized, at least vaguely, as an influential leader in the Church of England, a nationally distinguished scholar increasingly attended to abroad, and a man of considerable experience already in his middle years. Incongruity intensified when he was sent to Rome to study with youthful beginners in a seminary that prepared clergy for "mission" lands, among which Britain was still included. Well-intentioned efforts made in Rome to provide special accommodations for this anomaly – including makeshift private quarters and even scheduled servings of tea in deference to British taste – though amusing to imagine, were humiliating to experience.

Nor were matters improved when the classes provided for Newman's theological improvement proved to be intellectually vacuous.

For the Latin text of this work, see T. Lynch, "Textus nunc primo editus: The Newman-Perrone Paper on Development," *Gregorianum* 16 (1935), 402-447.

1

All such embarrassments, however, Newman was evidently ready to endure without protest as a providentially allotted exercise in humility. Only in diaries and private messages to friends does one perceive his sensitivity to the absurdity of it all. But it was a different matter when doubts arose concerning Newman's theological orthodoxy. Allowing himself to look silly might be commendable as meekness, but allowing himself to look heterodox would be irresponsible. Especially distressing were reported doubts regarding the orthodoxy of that very theological undertaking that had brought him into the Roman Catholic Church and which he hoped might prompt others to follow. Even in this matter Newman was resigned, but what he was resigned to was either an official repudiation of his position or a scholarly refutation of it. What he was not resigned to was a whispering campaign of skepticism, suspicion, and misrepresentation, evidently audible in the highest official circles, yet never presented openly as straightforward criticism. Newman had submitted his work unreservedly to ecclesiastical censorship. He would gladly have responded to scholarly critiques. But he could neither respect nor address mere insinuations or rumors of privately expressed disapprobation. He had learned even that his teaching on development was referred to disapprovingly by theology professors in Roman lecture halls. And he was aware that his critics did not base their opinions on a serious analysis of his writings, but on crude summaries, selective paraphrases, fragmentary translations, and mere hearsay. And he rightly surmised that a main excuse for such negligence was the sheer foreignness of his work, not only its English language, but its Anglican, Oxonian style, and historical scholarship uncongenial to the neo-Scholastic abstractness predominant in Roman theology.

One possible remedy that suggested itself to Newman was to try conveying the gist of his controversial views on development in an idiom more accessible to Roman academics, if he could only find among them some willing reader both competent and unprejudiced. Since Newman had only a bare smattering of Italian, he undertook to present in Latin a compendium of his doctrine, adopting as far as he could, Scholastic usages and categories. The result was a kind of abridged version, "in Roman Catholic," of his *Essay on the Development of Christian Doctrine.* He gave it the appropriately modified title, *De Catholici dogmatis evolutione* ("On the Development of Catholic Dogma"). Getting someone to read it with both intellectual sympathy and critical competence, who was believably representative of Roman theological scholarship, was not easy.

Newman had become persuaded that, despite the generally dreary state of theology and philosophy among the principal religious orders, greatest promise was to be found among the Jesuits. During Newman's sojourn in Rome he became aware of two Jesuit professors of theology who enjoyed unusual acclaim, as well as a reputation for considerable influence with Pope Pius IX. Of the younger of these, Carlo Passaglia, Newman had already heard that his disdain for Newman's views on doctrinal development was well-known in Roman circles, though never broached to Newman himself. Passaglia's antipathy for Newman's theology persisted in later years and probably diminished Newman's credibility at the papal curia. Rather amazingly, this defender of the faith who enjoyed the confidence of so censorious a pope, ultimately abandoned the Jesuits, the priesthood, and the Church itself to join the anti-papal forces of Italy's *Risorgimento.*

The other chief Jesuit luminary in Roman theology, who later became papal theologian, was Giovanni Perrone, an older man, author of many substantial and prestigious works, and professor of Dogmatic Theology at the Roman College, later given its present title, the Gregorian

University. Perrone had paid serious attention to Anglican and Protestant theology and was even acquainted with the uniquely modern Catholic theology currently appearing in Germany. Here, it must have seemed to Newman, was a man whose undoubted erudition combined depth with breadth, and yet whose Roman cultural and theological credentials seemed unexceptionable. He was, however, an intensely busy man, with many official employments, and Newman was especially gratified by his agreement to read and criticise the document Newman prepared. Newman left wide margins in his manuscript to accommodate any annotations Perrone saw fit to make, and the Jesuit inserted a number of brief comments. There is a winsome contrast between Perrone's crisp, workmanlike Latinity and Newman's vaguely Ciceronian prose patched with approximations of Scholastic jargon. As the comments reveal, Perrone read the work sympathetically and perceptively and criticized it with amiable candor. What the comments do not even suggest is the very warm esteem for Newman that took root at this time and continued to grow during subsequent years during which there was no personal contact between the two men. The best evidence of this is a letter, translated here as an appendix to the translation of Newman's Latin document, that Perrone wrote to Newman in Italian twenty years later, at a time when Newman had been much maligned in official Catholic circles. Perrone, aware of Newman's situation, not only declared his personal affection, but assured Newman that he had always been and would continue to be his staunch defender against critics. How deeply Newman was touched by that revelation of so lasting, active, and selfless a friendship is evident in his reply, here translated from the Latin. It is very probable that Newman owed much more to Perrone than a critical reading of his paper on the development of Catholic dogma.

As compared with Newman's Anglican writings on development this work is notably more abstract, containing less psychological and historical analysis, and more of an ecclesiological nature. It has overtones of Scholasticism, but is not a Scholastic exposition. Its references to post-Reformation writers omit favorite Anglican theologians in favor of Roman Catholics, and Perrone himself is cited frequently. Among patristic references, Latin writers, especially Augustine, are more prominent than is usual with Newman, who strongly preferred the Alexandrians. Scholastic references favor sixteenth century Counter-Reformation Jesuit Thomists, including significantly Francisco Suarez, whose writings against Anglican doctrine had been publicly burnt in the city of London. Newman takes as his general topic "the Word of God," that is, divine revelation or "Gospel truth." which he distinguishes as "objective" or "subjective." As objective it is given once and for all, simple and integral, existing as such in the mind of God, but also communicated to the Apostles and to the Church where it is the foundation of dogma. This is the Word of God "in itself" or absolutely, hence unchangeable. This conception of revelation, viewing it as a kind of Platonic transcendent reality, is congenial to neo-Platonic habits of thought shared by Newman and by Thomas Aquinas and his Scholastic followers. Given that "development," as Newman understands it, entails fundamental identity and continuity, the "objective" Word of God guarantees that permanence.

Newman at this point interjects a note, acknowledging his own ignorance of how the Church, as it were, taps the divine well of absolute truth so as to produce timely definitions of dogma. Is it by divinely assisted recourse to an unfailing tradition? Or is it by a supernatural empowerment of the Roman See to arrive simply and immediately at right answers to controversial questions of doctrine. Newman would probably favor the former interpretation, but he does not know the Roman Catholic answer to this question. It is noteworthy that this, the one direct question Newman inserts into his text, receives not even the hint of an answer in Perrone's annotations.

The complementary aspect of development is furnished by the "subjective" Word of God, that is, divine revelation as grasped, partially and distinctively, by each individual believer in her or his peculiar situation of time, place, and innumerable circumstances. Here, evidently, there is room for great variety and ceaseless change. Readers of Newman may recall how the notion of multifaceted truth, variously perceived and gradually integrated, underlies his philosophy of education. To describe the development of doctrine as part of the Church's progressive education would not be uncongenial to Newman's thought.

Though limited by individual finitude, the subjective Word of God is also enriched by qualities of personality, acquiring variety, spontaneity, and feeling in its apprehension and expression. And because God's Word is in itself integral, the grasping of any authentic part of it disposes the believer to receive more. At the same time, to focus over-narrowly on particular aspects may render other aspects less visible. On the whole, the religious knowledge of a devout believer tends to increase both in amplitude and in organization. This growth is fostered by many factors, not least of which is preaching. It does not depend on any strictly formal logic, though logic can and does play a part. Maintenance of coherence and equilibrium among various elements of belief is attributed to what Newman understands by the Pauline phrase, "analogy of faith." Nevertheless, the expansion of a believer's mind, while normal and wholesome, is not unerring. Inadvertence, exaggeration, and misapprehension occur inevitably and innocently. Innocence is lost only if correction by the Church is resisted, as in the case of heretics.

When correction by the Church takes the form of dogmatic definition, the subjective Word of God is brought into contact, so to speak, and into conformity with the objective Word of God. On such occasions the teaching Church does not only apply truth which it possesses; it can also discover explicitly, truth which it held hitherto only implicitly. There is therefore a sense in which the teaching Church may learn in the very process of teaching, just as students' difficulties may elicit from a teacher some clarifying insight not previously articulated or reflected upon, yet evidently in some sense already possessed. Newman attempts to illustrate this process with a generalized historical sketch of how a heresy might arise, win adherents, stir bishops to theological consultation, generate partisan controversy, elicit papal intervention, evoke conciliar study and constructive debate, and conclude with a dogmatic definition. Here Newman is clearly drawing on his historical studies of the Arian controversy to construct a historical model. Perrone, in his annotations, takes exception to Newman's account and offers one of his own in which the Pope, not a Council, has the decisive part.

Although this short work of Newman's occupies four chapters, the fourth is considerably longer than the preceding taken together. This final chapter begins with a set of twelve "theses," each of which is then defended in turn. It is in this argumentation that we find Newman marshalling, in support of his view, selected teachings of theologians respected as authorities in Roman Catholic circles.

In these theses, Newman contends that the initial deposit of faith was not a collection of distinct propositions, but rather distinct dogmatic formulations which emerged over the course of time. In that sense it might be possible to say the deposit has been added to. But since the additions emerged from what was already there, the resulting growth occurs without any real innovation. Nonetheless, dogmas thus brought to light, although not newly revealed, may still be newly perceived, as one may experience new awareness of implications not previously made explicit. Hence the uncertainty, caution, and contention that often accompany the coming to be of a new dogmatic definition. Hence too, the occurrence of genuine errors even among teachers of unimpeachable orthodoxy, which invite correction by later generations. Until attention is sharpened by controversy, such matters may be concealed by benign interpretations. Once a dogma has been defined, greater rigor is exercised to exclude opinions inconsistent with it. In all these matters, although endowed with infallibility, the Church proceeds under the Holy Spirit's guidance in a timely way. And at such times persons who are impatient of deliberation and insensitive to timeliness are prone to fall into heresy. Perrone's notes on these theses introduce some sharp notes of disagreement. These are, however, concentrated at the beginning of the chapter, and it may be that continued reading proved reassuring about initial misgivings. Mainly, Perrone's hesitations have to do with expressions of Newman's that might seem to qualify the insistence that the Church knew, from the very start, the whole of the revelation. It is clear enough that Newman emphasizes the process of doctrinal development, whereas Perrone emphasizes the permanence of doctrinal content. Yet neither seems to deny or misunderstand what the other stresses, and there is clearly a large area of mutual agreement. Perrone's final comment, after Newman's Thesis 12, summarizes his basic position. It contains four propositions, none of which are contradicted by Newman's teaching on development either here or in his earlier writings. Overall, the two men's positions appear to assume different slants while sharing the same foundation. Perrone's later testimony is hardly compatible with serious reservations about Newman's Roman Catholic orthodoxy.

WHETHER OR NOT THE CATHOLIC CHURCH MADE PROGRESS IN HER KNOWLEDGE OF THE FAITH ONCE DELIVERED TO HER BY THE APOSTLES

To Reverend Father Perrone, S.J.:

I am here sending you, most distinguished Sir, what, with characteristic kindness, you invited me to send. I fear you will find it even longer than you so patiently anticipated. It is most difficult, however, in even an extended treatise, to deal adequately with a matter which, although simple in itself, is obscure and unfamiliar. When you have some leisure, if indeed you ever get any, I could profit greatly from some marginal annotations indicating your critical reflections on these pages of mine. I hope I have not fallen into error. Still, with this kind of material it is much easier to hope than to be sure. I shall only declare, most emphatically, that although "I may err, I have no wish to be a heretic."

Yours respectfully &c
J. H. Newman

On the Development of Catholic Dogma

Chapter 1

On the Objective Word of God

1. The revealed word of God is that gift of Gospel truth, or deposit of faith, given in its fullness by Christ to his Apostles and by his Apostles to the Church, and transmitted whole and entire through the ages, even to the final consummation.(1)

2. That simple, absolute, immutable character, which is most truly found in the revealed word, belongs to it, however, only as considered *in itself*, or *objectively*, or in the form of dogma. It is quite otherwise when we consider it as a subject for human minds. For then it is a kind of *epinoia* of the one who receives it, involving parts, or aspects. There may be more to it or less. It has an initial phase. It grows. It improves.(2)

3. Since, however, all words are words of some speaker who enunciates them, and signify what is meant by those who express them, the word of God cannot be regarded otherwise than as present in some intellect, in a way that does not detract from its integrity and fullness, nor inject any alien taint into the natural luster of divine realities.(3)

4. Hence the word of God is said to be objective in the first instance as existing in the intellect of the Holy Spirit, to whom, as its supreme author and giver, the whole revelation is in every respect entirely manifest.(4)

5. It is likewise objective as existing in the intellect of the Apostles, fully illuminated by that Spirit who teaches them all truth.

6. Furthermore, according to the best authorities, the word of God is considered objective as, by a singular gift, always present in the intellect of the Church of Rome, where Peter is.(5) To that Church the faithful have constant recourse, drawing from it, for their own uses, truth itself.

N.B. The one thing I am doubtful about in this connection is whether it is a simple *tradition* in the Church of Rome, or a *faculty* possessed by the Roman See, whereby in the midst of the world's various and confused traditions and opinions, it can establish infallibly, in every question where the case requires just what is the truth confided by Christ to the Apostles.

7. With respect to the Catholic Church spread throughout the world, God's word has two aspects. In part it is subjective and in part objective.(6) It is to be termed objective insofar as it has been, and will continue to be transmitted, from Christ, from the Apostles, from the Supreme Pontiff, from Ecumenical Council in dogmas. But everything that has been everywhere handed down unanimously(7), not by design or in virtue of any definition, but freely and spontaneously, with depth of feeling(8) and variety of expression, is subjective to the mind of Catholics. More will be said of this presently, after considering the word of God as entertained in individual minds.

Perrone's Notes on Chapter 1

(1) This is evidently restricted to the New Testament.

(2) Moehler has written very well in his *Symbolik* about this subjective sense. It is termed subjective as being received in a subject, becoming something of our own.

(3) What is objective with regard to us is at the same time subjective with regard to God who utters the word. There is no problem here.

(4) I should prefer to say, in the divine intellect.

(5) In *the intellect of the Church of Rome.* I am not aware that this phrasing is in use. I should rather say *fully known to the Church of Rome.*

(6) These do not seem as though they should be linked together simultaneously. Instead I should say, *insofar as the Church and the Roman Pontiffs, taught by Christ and his Apostles, through dogmatic definitions when required,* etc.

(7) *Unanimously,* I should rather say *universally,* or *as held everywhere,* etc.

(8) I should say, *felt with a certain depth.*

Chapter 2

On the Subjective Word of God

1. The word of God is properly called subjective insofar as the faith once delivered by the Apostles to the Saints has its abode(1) in the minds of individuals, private persons, teachers, or churches of particular times or places.(2)

2. Even though the word of God has parts, those parts are not thrown together randomly but constitute a single whole.(3) Their coherence and consistency are such that all together comprise one totality. They mutually correspond. Each of them calls for the others. Deprived of the others, each would be emptied and enfeebled.(4)

3. It thus comes about that, in receiving one part, all are received.(5) Not as though one bare proposition once accepted has the power to draw the others after it, but because a person who is said to have embraced a dogma holds it in such a way(6) that all the others already have, at least potentially, or virtually, or dispositively, or inchoately, a foundation in that person's mind. For that Spirit in which the word is a totality lives in all its parts, but is communicated through each singly.(7) Nevertheless, the word is only truly received when it is received as delivered by the one who transmits it.

4. There is no other way, apart from a special gift, whereby anyone's mind could embrace the entire word of God. For the scope of any human intellect, even one of the greatest capacity, is far exceeded by the whole of that matter which the deposit of faith contains. For, many-sided, varied, and vast as it is, the mind of whoever contemplates it, while focussed

upon one point, commonly finds its view of some other point becoming blurred.(8) Accordingly, there are various ways of apprehending the divine word, corresponding to a variety of dispositions. They move from one point to another in different directions. And different minds find different starting points from which to revolve about a universe of doctrine, over a path that cannot be traversed in single lifetime.

5. Speaking in this way we have not overlooked the fact that, ordinarily, the faithful arrive at Catholic truth with assistanc from preachers and catechists. For after having earnestly embraced the articles of the creed, lively minds illuminated by divine light still have scope for personal inquiry. Then, without setting aside the magisterium, but under the permanent guidance of external authority, the word of God by its own vital power extends to some extent into its parts, attaining over the course of time its full amplitude.(9)

6. That is what is likely to happen whenever a mind both religious and acute devotes itself to meditating upon sacred things, or exploring the Scriptures, or combating heretics, or assisting believers. That is what we find outstandingly among the teachers of the Church. An initial vision of truth, commended to faith through hearing, although certain and efficacious in itself, is likely at first to be inchoate and unsteady, occupying the intellect in such a way as to weaken sometimes and waver, lacking sufficient control to find suitable verbal expression.(10) But when one contemplates it with a steady gaze, it often illuminates and attaches to the mind, winning free from a confused welter of thoughts with its parts clear and distinct, and taking on the character of a habitual disposition. Then it is alive and active in the intellect, no longer as a shadow of truth but as a reality, with its own foundation and properties. And it impresses upon the intellect an abundant knowledge of itself, what it is, what it is like, what are its constituent parts, how they are related to one another, what are their consequences, and how it relates to external matters,

physical, social, historical, philosophical. It shows, moreover, which of its parts are certain and which claim only the force of probability, what is the best way of relating them to one another and combining them into a totality. It shows what are the basic elements of that totality, the true ways of presenting it, the words by which those elements can be impressed deeply on human beings' understanding, the kind of rhetoric that avails against adversaries, what might be generally conceded, what is a firm standpoint, and what aspect is most congenially put forward.

7. What the intellect discovers as it turns and sifts matters in this way does not necessarily require any syllogistic equipment by which to establish premises and draw safe conclusions. It is by a freer mode of thought and a subtler procedure that the mind moves forward investigating and determining, often with little consciousness of how it is occupied and what it is learning. It is more like turning a light to illuminate some region that lies ahead, than fashioning and constructing something that, before one set to work, had not been there at all.

8. Not that the methods of logicians will not be put to use in treating a matter with others.(11) For them it is not a matter of the mind's growing in knowledge peacefully, quietly, and spontaneously. It is rather a deliberate stirring up of the matter, questioning and counter-questioning, and defending what is arrived at. That is how disputes arise among different schools, with different theologians choosing to go different ways, some dubious or fallacious, to coordinate different aspects of Catholic truth, or dissolve perplexities, or find apt words to express points of agreement.

9. Errors commonly occur, not in minor respects only but in major ones also, when the minds of private individuals, however learned and acute, occupy themselves unrestrainedly with matters of such gravity.(12) For whenever the intellect, relying on its own native resources or enticed by some philosophy, gives disproportionate emphasis to some part of

Catholic tradition, however valid in itself, it first disturbs the coordination of the parts. It then proceeds to derive from the parts it overemphasized implications that are ill-adjusted to other parts of the same tradition. Therein lies almost the whole force of heresy, for those who have erred seriously in theology are found more blameworthy for their denials than for what they affirm. (13)

That is why in every theological undertaking account must be taken of what is called the analogy of faith. For as we proceed in our reasonings, it functions like the Lydian stone, testing and examining how far it is clear, and whether or not the argument follows a legitimate course.

10. Moreover, not even a quite serious error in theology can be imputed as guilty or sinful to one who commits it, nor can it be more than materially heretical, unless it is maintained in opposition to what the Church declares or had previously declared. On the other hand, those who contradict definitions based on infallible authority show that really they do not even hold what they profess in explicitly Catholic terms.

Perrone's Notes on Chapter 2

(1) *Has its abode,* I should say, *is present in each one's mind in every age and place,* etc.

(2) Again, I should rather say, *is present in the Church's members, sensibly, luminously,* etc.

(3) In unitary fashion.

(4) An integral system, so compact and interwoven that the parts have a certain mutual interdependence, weakened by the deficiency of any part like a chain of joined links holding one another together, etc.

(5) Undividedly.

(6) On account of the same formal motive, etc.

(7) In unitary fashion or in entirety they possess the truth as transmitted by the Church.

(8) There should be no confusing what God has expressly revealed with what is contained therein implicitly, and can be developed and inferred in various circumstances. It is not difficult, especially under the Church's magisterium, to know what is expressly revealed. But it is decidedly difficult to grasp all that is necessarily connected with that. Over the course of time this is opportunely declared, in particular circumstances, by the Church's magisterium. For the Church is not only a depository and witness of divine revelation, but also an infallible judge in matters of controversy.

(9) Refer here again to what was remarked just above.

(10) Truths held formerly or initially in what may be called a confused state with regard to the substance of a matter, acquire greater definiteness through new formulations, and are proposed with clarity and distinctness. The Fathers, especially Augustine, bring this out repeatedly in the case of heresies. Having abused the general account put forward in the vigor of simple faith, these heresies compelled the Church to expose heretical deceits, and to equip the faithful with more precise formulations as safeguards against error.

(11) This would be called scientific method whereby reasoning from the principles of faith brings to light their latent implications.

(12) Moreover, matters of faith should not be confused with science, for it is sometimes uncertain in its procedures, whereas they are certain.

(13) Here we must distinguish a twofold function of theologians, as witnessing, and as teaching. As witnesses they set forth what the Church thinks. As teachers, however, they draw inferences, and in doing so they may make mistakes or be deceived.

Chapter 3

On the Subjective Word of God in the Catholic Church

1. Since it is only with the passage of time that the word of God passes into dogmas and becomes objective,(1) and is subjective in the Church insofar as it is not yet dogmatic, it follows that the word, as subjective to the Catholic mind, has precisely the same condition and history in the Church as it has in particular teachers, schools, and churches, as indicated in chapter 2.(2)

2. Initially the word of God enters the mind of the Catholic world through the ears of faith.(3) It penetrates that mind, recedes inside it, and remains hidden there, becoming a kind of deep internal sense. Quite inconspicuous, it is nonetheless very powerful. It is brought into play by the ministering and teaching Church. Its parts are distinguished and arranged; it is given shape, strengthened by tests, and applied as the nature of the case requires.(4) It goes through alterations, displaying different complexions and different leanings in accordance with different ages. In its manifestations it resembles ideas occupying the mind of some philosopher who, over the course of many years, ponders them, discusses them, and brings them to maturity.

3. The progress of the subjective word in the Catholic mind can be discerned – not only in disputations, controversies, and doctrines of former times, but also in the line of dogmas considered in itself, wherein, as one follows upon another, the word has already become to a great extent objective.(5) This does not occur randomly, but proceeds with a definite

order, as a kind of development having laws of its own and a history of its own.(6)

4. But until the Church has given dogmatic form to some part of its deposit, it may not yet be fully conscious of what it really thinks.(7) In that sense the Church, even though possessing the whole deposit of faith from the very beginning, can be said to have more theological knowledge now than it did in former ages.

5. The means by which the Church's subjective sense passes into objective dogmas are, in the first place, declarations by the Supreme Pontiff when he speaks *ex cathedra,* and secondly, definitions by ecumenical councils.(8)

6. Although the development of dogmas takes place in a quite similar way in the mind of an individual teacher and in the Catholic Church, the Church has, by a gift of Almighty God, something special and indeed unique. In the first place, when it speaks either in the person of the Supreme Pontiff or through an ecumenical council, it is strictly infallible and its dogmas altogether irreformable, even as the objective word itself entrusted to it by the Apostles. In the second place, even in matters it has not defined, but which are held everywhere and will continue to be held, it has a kind of presumptive infallibility which obliges all minds to accept them as certain, until such time as the Pontiff or a council pronounces on the matters more pointedly.(9)

7. If we wish to illustrate how, in fact, during the history of the Church, the subjective word becomes objective, let us call to mind what usually occurred from the time when a new heresy arose until its condemnation by the Pontiff. Suddenly faced with the proposition of some heresiarch, the bishops' minds are at first dismayed, and they do not see clearly how they should respond.(10) In virtue of that internal sense of the subjective word dwelling within them they recoil from the proposition and reject it. They turn to the dogmas of faith,

attend to the Scriptures, and consult the Fathers. Quickly, in accordance with the nature of the case, they assemble their ammunition. But meanwhile, faithlessness already latent in the Church consolidates itself, maps its own ground, and emerges as a faction. Some move into the heretics' camp. Others vacillate. Many, in their naivete, are misled for a time. The controversy grows more serious. Appeal is made to Peter, asking him to pronounce on the case. A council is assembled. Then the matter is disposed of peacefully. Opinions are advanced and questions are raised from all sides. Different views of the council fathers are elucidated or eliminated. Dogmas of faith already accepted are examined straightforwardly and at length. These become the seeds from which an apostolic definition grows that deals with the matter at hand. Finally, under God's direction and at his silent bidding, after a hard birth a new dogma comes into being.(11)

Perrone's Notes on Chapter 3

(1) This does not seem to be stated accurately. The word of God always, or from its conferral, passes into dogma or constitutes the object of our faith.

(2) Truths contained in it are not expressly or explicitly proposed as dogmas until they are defined by the Church and put forward expressly to be believed. That usually happens, however, with the rising of heresies injurious to truths that had been already previously implicitly believed.

(3) *Ears of faith.* What Paul said was: *faith through hearing – but hearing through the word of God.*

(4) This seems too ambiguous. The word of God remains immutable in itself, but with respect to us, as events require, the Church expounds the truth it contains in more narrowly defined formulations, as has been said.

(5) Divinely revealed truths evolve more and more, aided by learning or by reflection.

(6) For the reason I explained.

(7) I should not be so bold as to say that.

(8) These have contributed to further evolution.

(9) Presumptive infallibility cannot be admitted, for it is positive and real.

(10) The process is not like that, but quite the contrary. When a heresy or controversy arises it is initially debated among theologians of the region where the affair takes place. Bishops take it under consideration and submit it to the Roman Pontiff. He pronounces on it definitively. Ordinarily, the Pontiff's definition is the very last seal to be set upon a truth.

(11) It is not the case that a new dogma arises. Rather, by a new definition an old truth is put forward for explicit belief.

Chapter 4

Theses on the Word of God Made Manifest Through the Church

In order to clarify what it is I am proposing, I shall set forth in order a series of theses dealing with the whole matter, and afterwards I shall offer reasons to support them.

1. In the deposit of faith entrusted to the Church by the apostles there did not exist a definite number of articles to be transmitted, to which it was forbidden to make any additions. Rather, a series of dogmas, taught by pastors and learned by the faithful, grew up over the years, and continues to grow. (1)

2. Those dogmas which in former times the Church did not teach, but afterwards does teach, are not simply minor details. Rather they are serious matters, in virtue of their own inherent force and that of their situation. (2)

3. That the course of time adds some increment to the deposit is not a matter of chance. It follows an invisible ordinance of God and is regulated by certain laws. That is what the Councils discern when, while exercising human means, they are divinely guided to an irreformable conclusion. (3)

4. Of these norms what is most important is that whatever additions are made to the deposit are not really new, but evolved out of what is already there. (4) So Christian dogma really grows, rather than accumulates; there is no new beginning of truth, but the continuance of a real tradition. (5)

5. Even though the dogmas which come into being over the course of time are not really new in themselves, they may still be new to the Church of those times in which their form is evolving.(6) For one does experience as new what is implicit in what one already holds, as long as one has not yet become aware of the implication.

6. It is no wonder that, before dogmas are established, even Catholic writers should view them with some uncertainty and confusion, with the result that not only their statements but even their thoughts about them are quite wrong.(7)

7. Never have there been writers, or an age, or a span of ages, so disposed that their opinions about matters of faith in dogmas not yet promulgated left nothing to be corrected by succeeding generations.(8)

8. Until the mind of the Church on a given matter is about to be translated into dogma, the matter is not usually an object of attentive and painstaking contemplation.(9)

9. Thus it will happen, and fittingly enough, that since truth is one, and given to the Church from the beginning, even those not quite Catholic things that Catholics have brought forth, will generally strike so uncertain and ambiguous a note that, in any serious matter, they prove amenable to pious interpretation.(10)

10. Once a dogma has finally been formulated in words, there is no more place for dullness of understanding or ambiguity of expression on the part of the faithful.(11)

11. Even though the Church is enabled, whenever it defines a matter in dogmatic form, to exercise infallibility, it nevertheless proceeds in a timely way to issue its definition, sooner or later, whenever it is willed by that Spirit in whom it is infallible.(12)

12. Presumptuous persons, who do not wait for the Church to speak, but want by dint of their own struggle to carry off

the truth about some matter prematurely, usually achieve not the truth they are seeking, but heresy. (13)

Perrone's Notes on Chapter 4

(1) If you mean *formulated* dogmas, there were certainly few of them, if any. But if you mean truths considered in themselves, contained severally in the deposit, then there have been no additions.

(2) I do not understand what is meant by these *minor details.*

(3) We should rather express it as divine *assistance.*

(4) The deposit is not *expanded,* for it always remained unchangeable.

(5) Dogma does not grow *in itself.* But it does grow quantitatively in relation to us, evolving into greater explicitness and more distinct awareness of articles that have been defined.

(6) Only a sanction or formal definition is new.

(7) That may happen in the case of private individuals, but not of the Church.

(8) In the sense indicated above.

(9) That is to say, individuals may have no very profound mental grasp of it.

(10) In the sense already explained.

(11) Once they know, all must believe explicitly.

(12) Namely, as circumstances require.

(13) It is not for that reason, but because they rashly introduce novelties contrary to what is held in the Church or to what the Church teaches.

Thesis One

In the deposit of faith entrusted to the Church by the apostles there did not exist a definite number of articles to be transmitted, to which it was forbidden to make any additions. Rather, a series of dogmas, taught by pastors and learned by the faithful, grew up over the years, and continues to grow.(1)

Augustine repeatedly observes that, "hidden among God's people there were many quite capable of analyzing and treating the Scriptures. They did not expound solutions of *difficult questions* simply because there was no present threat from any deceiving pretender. The Trinity was not *fully* treated until the Arians came ranting about it. Neither was penance *fully* treated &c. Nor was there *entire clarity* even about the unity of Christ &c." (Psalm 54, 22)(2)

"There must therefore be growth and vigorous progress in *understanding, knowledge,* and wisdom, on the part of each and all, of individual persons and of the whole Church." (Vincent. Comm. 28)(3)

"The Holy Spirit has always been accustomed," writes Suarez, "*to teach* concerning all that pertains to supernatural doctrine, not all at once, but *at opportune times,* according to the disposition of his hidden providence. This can be seen in antiquity, for, leaving aside the era of natural law, sacred doctrine grew over the course of time even in the synagogue, as God sent prophets at various junctures. Moreover, since, despite the Scriptures, doubts and ambiguities still arose, God established a place for a priestly tribunal whence the people could obtain progressive enlightenment about divine matters. Even in the primitive Church not everything was taught to the apostles at once by the Holy Spirit. Peter was only later instructed about the call of the Gentiles (Acts 10). And the Church was made more sure about the cessation of legal obligations at the Apostolic Council than it had been before. Thus, *after the time of the apostles* the Church was able to gain *enlightenment about many things* that might prove *necessary* at later times but were not so before. It might be on account of doubts newly raised, especially by insurgent heretics or other presumptuous persons, offering false interpretations of obscure matters of faith. It might also be because the *natural human condition* of making gradual progress in *knowledge* is one that God wished to be found also in his Church &c." (de Anglic. Sect. I. 18 #4)

"It could not, or certainly at least should not happen that the whole of theological doctrine, so to speak, taught by the Holy Spirit to the apostles, was transmitted to the Church or taught to others *in the same way,* rather than in the way best suited to the occasion. So it was not necessary for *all the truths,* or conclusions drawn from them, to be *distinctly transmitted* or declared. Or perhaps many things pertaining to a fuller explanation and subtler *knowledge* of the articles of faith were taught verbally, but afterwards came into doubt, either on account of some heresy or, sometimes, *on account of ignorance,* as in fact is confirmed by Cyprian in letter 74 and others &c." (ibid #7)

"Although revelation is the meaning of Sacred Scripture, in her knowledge of which the Church cannot err, it *is nevertheless not revealed* that that meaning is well rendered and expressed by our vulgate version, a question of fact. Yet the Church at the Council of Trent *declared* that version to be authentic and free of any errors contrary to faith." (Tournely de Eccles., p. 256)

"Errors come to wake the Church up, and make her *understand* better what she believes." (Bossuet Instr. Past. I #34)

"One believes in virtue of the Church's faith; one understands with the help of more particular explanations furnished by the holy Doctors. Thus, seeing little children baptized, one believes, in all simplicity, that they are sinners, because it is remission of sins that baptism bestows on them. That truth comes to be disputed by a heresy, and then one *develops* with greater clarity St. Paul's teaching about the two Adams." (&c #35)

"It is clear that the famous saying of Vincent of Lerins, 'What always &c' should be understood only in what is called a positive sense. That is, 'What always &c' could not fail to be true or to derive from apostolic tradition. But it should not be understood in a negative sense, as meaning that anything that was not 'always &c' believed, or at least explicitly believed, should not be regarded as true or certain. Otherwise that would have applied to the authenticity and canonicity of all the deuterocanonical writings, which is plainly absurd." (Perron. de Ver. Rel. p. 245 nota 1)

Perrone's Notes on Thesis One

(1) No truth grows. What do grow are the formal definitions of a truth once handed down.

(2) These are to be understood in the way previously indicated.

(3) Likewise.

Thesis Two

Those dogmas which in former times the Church did not teach, but afterwards does teach, are not simply minor details. (1) Rather they are serious matters, in virtue of their own inherent force and that of their situation.

This second thesis will be controversial, whereas the previous one expresses an almost universal consensus. (2) The very nature of the case makes it apparent that all truths of theology cannot be contained in a deposit of faith, however ample, in a series of treatises set down in writing, still less in doctrines orally transmitted by an older generation to the memory of a younger one.

This is sufficiently taken for granted among theologians that they freely add to God's word set forth in propositions, as elements of revelation, matters implicitly or logically latent therein. And this will suffice as long as full liberty is given, to assure that those implications and consequences of God's word emerge with their proper seriousness and magnitude. But it will not suffice if false limits are imposed. Suarez, indeed, in the passages already commended, likens dogmatic additions made to the Gospel to those that occurred in the Mosaic law, certainly describable as *implications* or *consequences* of those seminal elements originally given to the Hebrews, but in a less restricted sense which I hope to indicate in what follows. (3)

1. He calls attention to a clear example of this in the history of the Catholic Church. "The *truth* that persons properly baptized by heretics should not be re-baptized was sufficiently doubtful for Cyprian and a multitude of bishops to hold the

contrary opinion. Yet, afterwards it was defined by the Church in the Council of Carthage and other councils, which undoubtedly sufficed to establish certitude, as Augustine rightly teaches. (lib. 1. contr. Cresc. c. 32) Yet, even though this might appear to be a *new* doctrine, it is Apostolic doctrine, because it is virtually contained therein and not unknown to the apostles themselves. For they received the gift of the Holy Spirit who expounded all things to them, as explained by Epiphanius (Haer 66) and more fully by Tertullian (in Praescript). This is to be understood *not only with reference* to the day of Pentecost, however, for even after that they could, at opportune times, be instructed or illuminated about various matters." (de Sect. Anglican. I. 18. #7)

If the validity of the baptisms of heretics is to be considered, at least as far as I am concerned, as an implied or logical truth, I should say only that, given that fact, there are truths of such importance, not taught by the Church in former times, but taught later on. (4)

2. Additional examples are easy to find. On a major issue of controversy with the Lutherans, Vasquez writes as follows: "Problems concerning the formal cause of our justification tend to be the most difficult of all those having to do with justification. In past centuries they were not analyzed by the Fathers as thoroughly as were questions, still under debate, concerning the necessity of grace for righteous living." (Quaest. 112 Disp. 202, c. 1. init.)

Among non-Catholics, the learned Anglican scholar, Barrow, testifies from his own point of view how barren the field of ancient theology was concerning this matter. "Perhaps, as can be observed in their treatment of some other matters, here also the Fathers spoke less than accurately on a subject that had not been fully argued by their predecessors." (de Justif.)

3. Knowing the canon of the sacred books is scarcely a trivial matter. And yet it is recognized that this was not contained in

that deposit which the third century Catholic Church delivered to the faith of the following century.(5)

4. Moreover, there are many matters about which the holy Fathers could never have spoken as they did if they had already learned from the Church truths which are nowadays inculcated either in express terms or as implied in rituals and forms of worship. If the gifts and privileges of the Blessed Virgin Mary familiar to modern believers had been established as dogma, transmitted by the Eastern, Egyptian, and Gallican churches of the third and fourth centuries, how could Origen have said that Mary sinned during the Passion? (Chrysostom, in Matth. Hom. 44) How could he have called her "ambitious," saying that she wanted to show the people how she controlled and exercised authority over her son, because her own imagination had not envisaged for him anything very great." Indeed, if she found herself pregnant without understanding what was happening, she "would probably have taken her own life rather than be trapped under an unbearable burden of disgrace" (as Petavius puts it). According to Cyril, the Mother of the Lord was almost distraught at her son's unanticipated suffering, to the point of saying, 'The one I gave birth to is now being mocked upon a cross. Perhaps he was, after all, deluded in claiming to be the son of Him who rules all things.' " And Cyril goes on to say that there is nothing astonishing in this, since this suffering had to be endured by "the impressionable mind of a mere woman."

5. Nor, if the pre-Nicene church had expressly taught what we have in the Athanasian Creed, about the "incomprehensible Father, incomprehensible Son, etc.," would there have been any need for Bull vigorously to defend those centuries.

6. Who would deny that the Church could issue at this very time, if it chose to, a definition concerning indulgences?(6) And who would deny that the matters defined were not actually among the number of those that pastors now every-

where plainly teach as portions of dogmatic tradition, but were either local traditions or drawn from the inner recesses of the Catholic mind, where the Spirit filled with truth dwells, not compressed in formulae, but in particular circumstances made manifest in formulae?

7. Who would marvel if today's Church should define the essence of original sin, which the Fathers at Trent did not find a way of defining?

Other factors lead to similar inferences. Consider the august ritual of the Mass, given to the Church from the very beginning. Consider it as a reality, a fact set before one's eyes. Behold that marvelous action, handed down by the Apostles to those whom they had brought to the faith, performed daily, and frequented by believers everywhere. This was no bare dogma, but an act of worship. It is no verbal formula, but a solid, living institution. It has many parts and many aspects. It can be contemplated from every side. It must be pondered, studied, embraced by the mind, penetrated by the intellect, preserved in the memory. It is a mystic ritual where Christ appears as born into the world, hung upon the cross, clothed in a spiritual body, both victim and priest. It is a real and lasting presence, an efficacious action. It is a source of blessing and an object of adoration. It is propitiatory offering and it is food. It is for the living, and for the dead. It is a sacrament and a symbol, yet the very thing it signifies. It is the memorial of the Lord's death, but it is the Lord himself. It is living bread, yet not bread but flesh. It is a true sacrifice, yet a commemoration.(7) Who could not derive from this one source six hundred complete dogmas? And yet who could do so in a single century. much less by a single consideration of the mind?

Perrone's Notes on Thesis Two

(1) Whatever the Church teaches, it has always taught, even if in a different way, a way that may be more or less plain and explicit.

(2) On the contrary, it is denied by all Catholics. For all the truths are divinely transmitted to the Church's deposit in a unitary, consolidated fashion, even though it is only over the course of time that they unfold and become distinct propositions presented to our faith to be believed.

(3) I do not think that is what Suarez actually had in mind. Otherwise, he would be proving too much.

(4) In the sense explained.

(5) It was in the deposit; however it was not fully known to everybody.

(6) But this was defined by the Council of Trent in its twenty-fifth session.

(7) All these have always been held and professed by the Church.

Thesis Three

That the passage of time adds some increment to the deposit is not a matter of chance.(1) It follows an invisible ordinance of God, and is regulated by certain laws. That is what the Councils discern when, while exercising human means, they are divinely guided to an irreformable conclusion.(2) Two such laws are expounded by Suarez. (loc. cit. 1.18. 4 and 9) "In the first place, nothing is introduced that contradicts either divine positive law or natural law. Next, it all derives from that legitimate power which Christ bestowed on his Vicars and the Pastors of the Church." Such would be the case in discerning implications and consequences. If this were an occasion for disputation, I could treat this matter at greater length. Personally, I would propose at least seven norms to look for in addition to a dogma of faith that are to be regarded as legitimate.

Perrone's Notes on Thesis Three

(1) There is no intrinsic increment. The increment is only extrinsic, an increased number of articles to be believed explicitly.

(2) The human means serve only to deepen knowledge.

Thesis Four

The most important of these norms is that whatever additions are made to the deposit are not really new, but evolved out of what is already there. So Christian dogma really grows, rather than accumulates; there is no new beginning of truth, but the continuance of a real tradition.

"We say it is one thing to believe something repugnant to the dogmas and doctrines preached by the Apostles. It is quite another thing to believe something by way of addition to the doctrine the Apostles preached, something not expressly declared by them, or at least not demonstrated to have been so declared." (Suarez. 1. c. #3)

"Paul did not tell Timothy, I. 6, simply that novelties must be avoided, but 'profane novelties of language.' For, as St. Thomas remarks on that same text, not every novelty is objectionable, for the Lord did say, I give you a new commandment,' John 13, but only profane novelty, that is, novelty that opposes divine and sacred realities. Earlier, that had been Augustine's view, in Tract. 97 on John, near the end. One finds almost the same thing in Vincent of Lerins, c. 37, asking 'What is "profane"? that which has nothing of a sacred, of a religious character, completely alien to the inner depths of the Church which is God's temple, etc. Profane novelties of language, that is of dogmas, matters, thoughts which are contrary to antiquity.' By the same token, what are not contrary, but rather serve for a better understanding of antiquity, cannot be called profane novelties.(1) Indeed, they should not be called novelties at all, for they were contained in antiquity, and virtually, or as they say, implicitly, believed. When, later on, they are delivered in more explicit form, they should be characterized not as new things, but as old things newly expressed." (Ibid. #5)

Consider also those testimonies already presented in arguing the first thesis. For a general example, take the Church's faith concerning the Blessed Virgin Mary. The longer and the more closely Catholics meditated on the dogma of the Incarnation, the more apparent it became that esteem for the Son was involved in esteem for his Mother, to such an extent that loving and honoring the Son was not possible without loving and honoring the Mother as well. What is more, they found it an indispensable sign of right faith in the Incarnation of the Word to extol her through whom it came to pass. Thus the dogma of the dignity of the Mother of God arose not out of substantive tradition, but out of meditation. In treating a certain proposition of faith, Perrone observed that certain "Popes present clear statements of the Fathers, and examples of the saints collected by Bellarmine which, although not strictly conclusive, show nevertheless the Church's spirit, and the *seed* of this dogma in tradition which was later to *evolve*." (de Matrim p. 285) Here we see the dogma of faith, not in its fully matured form, but germinally, committed to tradition. Consider also de Eccles, p. 17, where, treating matters of dogma, he writes as follows: "Over the course of the ages the Church progressively evolves the *principles* and *seeds* implanted by Christ in its very foundation *as already authorized by the Apostles.*" He establishes that the *post*-Apostolic Church adopted a similar explanation of its own dogmas as though received from the living Apostles. See also p. 509, where he asserts that the Church had already possessed certain rights, even before actually exercizing them.

Perrone's Notes on Thesis Four

(1) This is all quite true if it is understood as indicated above.

Thesis Five

Even though the dogmas which come into being over the course of time are not really new in themselves, they may still be new to the Church of those times in which their form is evolving. For one does experience as new what is implicit in what one already holds, as long as one has not yet become aware of the implication.(1)

Consider the debate at the Council of Trent about Christ's offering himself in sacrifice at the supper, as reported by Pallavicini, xviii, 2. Salmeron's arguments proved so persuasive for many of the fathers who had previously opposed that teaching, that it found a place in the Council's doctrine. With regard to that dogma, did not those fathers, and indeed the Church of that time, make progress in knowledge of the deposit?

Pallavicini writes as follows: "Such was the outcome. Whereas in the beginning many were opposed to any kind of declaration of this offering of himself made there by Christ, what happened at the end was the very opposite of what usually occurs in subtle arguments. Usually, each individual, enamored of what his own ingenuity conceived, is confirmed in the position he took. But in this case nearly everybody swung over to the affirmative position, joining those whom they had most strenuously opposed." (n. 12)

Perrone's Notes on Thesis Five

(1) Not in themselves, but with respect to our *knowledge*.

Thesis Six

It is no wonder that before dogmas are established even Catholic writers should view them with some uncertainty and confusion, with the result that not only their statements but even their thoughts about them are quite wrong.

There is no lack of examples, some of which I shall cite here and others under different theses.

Two or three Catholic dogmas, and very important ones, were opposed by the martyr St. Cyprian. One was the validity of baptisms conferred by heretics. Another was the authority of tradition. Possibly a third, at least in practice, was the teaching authority of the Supreme Pontiff.

Not only Origen and Clement of Alexandria, but also Irenaeus and Gregory of Nyssa believed, or at least conjectured, that the devil would ultimately be restored to his place in heaven, or at least that the fire of hell would not be everlasting.

Hilary seems to have assigned the pains of Purgatory not to the interval between death and judgment, but to the time of judgment itself.

Trent defined that "The priest's sacramental absolution is a judicial act, not a mere ministry of declaring to one who confesses that his sins are forgiven." St. Bonaventure, however, seems to have held a quite different opinion. Pallavicini says of him that "intelligent persons should have no less esteem for that holy and glorious doctor. For they are aware that other very ancient and very holy doctors took up certain errors subsequently condemned by the Church, in condemning the Semiarians or Semipelagians, or in judging some deliberate deception, etc." (xii, 12)

Thesis Seven

Never have there been writers, or an age, or a span of ages, so disposed that their opinions about matters of faith in dogmas not yet promulgated left nothing to be corrected by succeeding generations.(1)

In the Maurist preface to St. Ambrose's treatise on "A Good Death," after noting what that holy Doctor had said about the state of souls, they write as follows: "It is no wonder that Ambrose should have written in that way about the state of souls. Yet it does seem almost incredible how unsure and inconsistent the holy Fathers remained on that subject all the way from the Apostolic age to the pontificate of Gregory XI and the Council of Florence, that is for nearly fourteen centuries. They did not only differ from one another, as tends to happen in questions not yet definitively settled by the Church. They were not even consistent with themselves, sometimes appearing to grant that the souls enjoy a clear vision of the divine nature, but elsewhere in their writings seeming to deny the very same thing.

"At least since the Council of Trent," writes Perrone, "it is close to a matter of faith that for properly receiving the Sacrament of Penance a contrition perfected in charity is not necessary." (de Poen. p. 417) "We are not unaware," he continues, that before Trent, at least until St. Thomas, it was often contended by the older scholastics that perfect contrition was necessary for fruitfully receiving the Sacrament of Penance, and that this was in fact their common doctrine." (Ibid. p. 440)

The same author, writing on the Sacrament of Orders, points out that "Countless ecclesiastical monuments can be cited on both sides, some affirming and others denying the validity of such ordinations (conferred by illegitimate ministers), since the matter had not yet been settled. Now the teaching of St. Thomas has prevailed for centuries, and gained the assent of the universal Church, to the effect that ordinations by heretics, schismatics, and simoniacs must be regarded as quite valid." (de Ordin, p. 157)

In another place in the same work: "Cardinal Raymond cites 80 authors who deny that the Episcopate is an order, etc. It is quite true, as Cano wrote, that no one should be overwhelmed by a sheer *number* of theologians. I should add that the same must be said of their *prestige*. For the negative opinion was defended not only by the Master of the Sentences, but also as we have seen by St. Thomas, as well as by St. Bonaventure, Scotus, Innocent V, Lessius, etc., etc." (p. 125, n. 1)

It certainly happens that, in the course of time, as occasioned by controversies or changed circumstances, there do appear new aspects, new arrangements, new hypotheses, and new analyses of major portions of the whole dogmatic structure. After Jansenism, in how different a light did the Church view no small part of the ethics of the Gospel! At first sight, how different are the views of original sin expressed by the Greek Fathers, Gnostic and Manichaean sectaries, and Pelagius' adversary, Augustine! How different are the arguments about fear advanced by ancient and modern teachers! How different modern Catholics sound when they speak of taking up the civil sword in matters of faith, from what was formerly heard on that same subject, if not in the schools of the doctors, at least among monks and bishops! Consider another kind of example, taken from Pallavicini: "We know how all those opinions were received from the scholastics in such a way that Ptolemy determined the system of the Universe – not because he had set out to *prove* that the Universe with all its spheres and stars was arranged and located in precisely that way; but only in order to propose *one possible way* which, if verified, would accommodate all the phenomena we actually observe in the heavens and on earth, even though countless other ways could have been discovered by God and Nature. . . . The "if" concerns the certitude of faith; the "what" pertains to the exercise of genius." (ix, 5)

Perrone's Notes on Thesis Seven

(1) This must be understood of particular, individual teachers.

Thesis Eight

Until the mind of the Church on a given matter is about to be translated into dogma, the matter is not usually an object of attentive and painstaking contemplation.

Why did the Tridentine theologians so anxiously scrutinize the works of the Fathers in arriving at their definitions? (See e.g. Pallav. Hist. viii, 4, n. 6.) It was not merely to confirm a certain tradition about matters under consideration, one that was already plain and clear to their minds. It was rather to enlighten their minds by reading and meditating about those matters. Which is contrary, I think, to what happened at Nicaea, where the tradition about the Son of God seems to have been more vivid in the minds of the Fathers than in the writings of their predecessors. What I conclude is that a particular tradition can certainly exist, not so much in the conscious mind or awakened intellect of the Church, and in a dogma of faith, as in virtue of a kind of germinal power belonging to what is already contained in dogma.(1)

We can see this illustrated and confirmed in what Augustine wrote about repeating the baptism of heretics. "How," he asks, "could this issue, wrapped as it was in such clouds of contention, be brought to an admirable clarification and confirmation by a plenary council, if it were not known to have been dealt with over a long period of time and in many parts of the world, and from different sides, in debates and episcopal conferences?" (de Baptism, ii. 4)(2)

The process we are considering, of thinking and acting about a serious matter that is not yet sufficiently stabilized, is shown by Dionysius of Alexandria in his dealings with the Supreme Pontiff of the same name. He, speaking rather freely about the nature and incarnation of the Son of God while pursuing the Sabellians, but afterwards recalled by the Pontiff to a sounder way of expressing himself, contemplated with a steady gaze the holy faith that had been delivered and entrusted to him. As a result he presently began, as befitted a Catholic leader, to speak in a Catholic manner. Here again we observe that knowledge of truth which is not yet a present, vivid intellectual vision, perfected by activity. Rather it is latent in the mind, preserved rather by memory than by habit, able, certainly, to be brought to light at the bidding of the will, but not an idea contemplated by the mind's eye, a power permeating all modes of thought and spontaneously expressed in words. Not that the mighty Confessor was in such a state that he did not, in the Apostle's words, "live by faith in the Son of God." On the contrary, faith was stronger in him than any intellectual contemplation of faith. And so it was with all those who lived before the Church had defined any article.

This is my interpretation of those ante-Nicene Fathers who spoke somewhat unsuitably about the Son of God, namely those, if any, who apparently held that the Word was not always the Son. (3) They were not consistent, but at the time they thought something or other that was contrary to their dogma. And they developed, in a defective way made inevitable by the nature of the case, what the Church had not yet developed with clarity.

I shall venture something more, perhaps audaciously. I am ready to retract it if it proves rash.

When the bread was called Flesh by the ancients, they were calling it precisely what it would later be called by the Council of Trent. Directly, as they say, it is Flesh. But indirectly it is concomitantly Flesh and more than Flesh. It is Blood, and Soul, and the whole Person of Christ, at once God and man. But it was as Flesh that the ancients viewed it, whereas, after further development, those of more recent times, because it was Flesh viewed it also as Blood. Those of more recent times did not on that account regard the faith of the ancients as incomplete.(4) They preserved it and they expanded it, but they expanded it only by what did it no injury, but perfected it. It is in that sense that the Church grows in its knowledge of dogmas. By handling very carefully what it possessed from the start, it enlarges its awareness of it.

Is it not in much the same sense that we must say that the structure of the Nicene Creed makes it clear that the Church issued that very ancient and sacred testimony of faith out of a mind that was less many-sidedly involved in divine knowledge than the one from which it was later to issue the Psalm *Quicumque* or Pius's profession of faith?

It is not as though the dogma of the Most Holy Trinity as we find it in the Psalm *Quicumque,* was not dwelling in the mind of the Church. But it was dwelling there as a kind of secondary aspect of a truth whose primary aspect was "One God, the Father Almighty; his consubstantial Son; the Spirit, Paraclete, who proceeds from the Father." Similarly, where the Apostolic Age preached "One God, One Mediator, Christ," since the time of Bellarmine we give "Praise to the Triune God and the Virgin Mother," not as though Christ had been displaced by his Mother, but because Christ is included in the Triune God and the Blessed Virgin is closely connected.

Are not the sacred ritual of the Mass and the rite of priestly ordination composed in a different way than they would have been if, during that ancient period, theological disciplines had been flourishing?

Perrone's Notes on Thesis Eight

(1) The Church always possessed and was conscious of the whole deposit of revelation entrusted to her, even if sometimes, when there was no dispute or contradiction, a certain truth might remain latent which later came out publicly.

(2) St. Augustine here confirms what I just stated.

(3) Among the ante-Nicene Fathers it seems that one can make a distinction between what was maintained in the Church and held by the Fathers themselves, and their way of expounding it according to the positions of philosophers, as Moehler points out with respect to Athanasius.

(4) Ancient writers sometimes used language by which they were plainly expressing what is stated by recent writers. Cf. Tractatus de Eucharistia, where it treats of the whole Christ under either of the two species.

Thesis Nine

Thus it will appear, and fittingly enough, that since truth is one, and given to the Church from the beginning, even those not quite Catholic things that Catholics have brought forth, will generally strike so uncertain and ambiguous a note that, in any serious matter, they prove amenable to pious interpretation.

One example should suffice for this thesis. It is well known among serious students of theology that some of the fourth century Fathers spoke of the knowledge of Christ's soul in such a way as to suggest that they did not believe it to have been perfect from the very moment of his conception in Mary's womb, but to have begun growing as he "advanced in age," as the Evangelist says. It is Catholic dogma that the man (or human nature) assumed by the Word did not have, abstractly speaking or in first act, as they say, perfect knowledge, but that really, or in second act, he did have it, because the man was deified in the Word. Thus Christ, as a man, would never have been ignorant of anything a man could know. As Gregory the Great expresses it "he knew *in* the nature but not *from* the nature of his humanity." (Ep. x. 39) What did Athanasius write, before the heretical Agnoetae arose, concerning the coming day of judgment? "That hour, in which all will end, he knew as the Word, but as a man he was ignorant of it For ignorance is a property of man." (orat. iii. contr. Arian. 43) Mindful of this and similar texts of Athanasius and others, Petavius writes: "Some Catholics, including some of great fame and distinction in the Church, attributed ignorance to the man Christ, especially ignorance about the final days and last judgment." Examples are "Athanasius, Eustathius of Antioch, Gregory Nazianzen, Cyril, Hilary, and Ambrose." A little further on, he adds the warning that this opinion, "although once acceptable to some very outstanding men, was later characterized as *heresy* and heretics condemned under that heading were called Agnoetae." (de Incarn. XI, 1, #5, 15)

But if we take a closer look at the texts of these Fathers we shall not find it difficult to interpret them in a Catholic sense. We need only attach a note to those texts to the effect that, being found in writings of those who came before the developed dogma of Christ's knowledge, they sketched the truth of the Gospel in broader lines. There are many reasons for believing that those Fathers, when they said that Christ, as man, was ignorant of the judgment day, meant that he was ignorant *from,* not *in* his human nature. That is, his ignorance was not real but only economic, as suited humanity in itself, or as suited the office or role he was undertaking, as when he asked "Where shall we buy bread for them to eat?" even though "He himself knew what he was going to do." For Athanasius writes that Christ's ignorance "does not pertain to the Word, but to human nature, of which ignorance is a property." (ibid.) "Since he was made man, he is not ashamed, on account of ignorant flesh, to say I do not know, thereby showing himself to be knowing as God, but not knowing according to the flesh." (ibid.) Again, "Let us acknowledge that the Word, not ignorant in so far as it was the Word, said I do not know, yet did indeed know.

But it was to display what is human, for ignorance is properly human and, having put on human flesh, since he was in it, he said, consistently with it, I do not know." (ibid., 45) "In order to teach that as a man he did not know, he said, Nor the Son." (ibid., 46) "He inquired, as a man, about Lazarus, even though he would go on to raise him from the dead."(ibid.) There is surely implied that even the man Christ knew about Lazarus. It does not matter that #47 compares Christ's ignorance to ignorance the Apostle admitted with regard to something he really did not know about at the time. For he goes on to write, "He did that, it seems to me, for our advantage." #48-50. (It happens that the very word "economically" is ambiguous in Basil where he discusses Christ's ignorance of the day of judgment. It refers to both the Lord's incarnation, Ep. 236. 1, and to that condescension whereby he accommodated himself to human understanding. (Ep. 8. 6) The same is true of Cyril, Trin. p. 623. Thesaur. p. 224. – (it is the same with the word "dispensation" in Hilary. (Trin. X. 8. ed. Maur.) In Ep. 8 Basil suggests that Christ "exercised an economy by pretended ignorance." Likewise Cyril, though he had previously said "Just as he received this, that being made a man he would share in men's hungering and thirsting, by the same token no one should object if, as a man in union with men he should say that he did not know." (Thesaur, p. 221) Shortly afterwards, moreover, he added that "The Son knew all things, even though saying economically that he did not know certain things." p. 224. And in Trin. iv. p. 629, he seems to point towards that distinction later made by Gregory the Great, according to which the man Christ was ignorant from the assumed nature, but not in that nature. Like Athanasius, he says "He professes ignorance *for our sake.*" (Thesaur., p. 221, 223) And Hilary who, if the text of Trin. ix, at the end, is genuine, established so plainly the ignorance of the man Christ, had only a short time before argued that the judgment day should be known to him as a man who, as a man, was himself the judge. "And since he is himself the Sacrament let us see if, in those things he does not know, he truly is ignorant." He also gives reasons for Christ's having professed not to know. 67. Namely (to use the words of Augustine), "Christ called himself unknowing concerning that in which, by concealment, he made others unknowing." (Ep. 180, 3) Or, as Augustine puts it in another place, "He is ignorant concerning that of which he makes ignorant." (de Trin. I. 23)

But that will suffice on this subject.

Thesis Ten

Once a dogma has finally been formulated in words, there is no more place for dullness of understanding or ambiguity of expression.

The definitions which, as being the Church's own voice, may not be contradicted, instruct and strengthen the faithful at the very same time that they impose an obligation on them. What they commend to faith as dogma, they impress upon the intellect as truth. Not as though they provided a verbal formula that clever persons who tacitly resist the Church could not possibly get around, or that put so firm an end to controversies that more adequate formulations might not be required in the course of time. All the same, such definitions wonderfully illuminate the matter and commend it to the minds of the faithful. They have their natural significance, even though it is not inseparably bound to a particular set of words. And if they do not absolutely abolish the controversies on which they bear, they do at least put them to rest for a very long time.

Thesis Eleven

Even though the Church is enabled, whenever it defines a matter in dogmatic form, to exercise infallibility, it still proceeds in a timely way to issue its definition, sooner or later, whenever it is willed by that Spirit in whom it is infallible.

The Church is infallible at the time when it speaks. But in God's design, there are many factors influencing whether it should speak at one time or another. In this respect the Church's teaching office differs from the schools of theologians, and from doctors, philosophers, and heretics, who are ready to publish their opinions, Catholic or not, whenever it happens to suit them. But that very readiness to dispute which characterizes private individuals furnishes the material out of which, after long deliberation, the Church fashions its defined teachings. As a result, since disputes will always arise among theologians, the Church's exercise of infallible judgment is a permanent and, as it were, provisional function. It is easy to find at the present time questions, not yet defined, that demand and await ecclesiastical judgment, such as the inspiration of the Scriptures, the infallibility of the Supreme Pontiff, the Immaculate Conception of the Blessed Virgin Mary, and others.

Thesis Twelve

Presumptuous persons, who do not wait for the Church to speak, but want by dint of their own struggle to carry off the truth about some matter prematurely, usually achieve not the truth they are seeking, but heresy.(1)

It would take me too long if I undertook fully to illustrate this thesis with examples. A few may suffice. Early heretics wanted to make use of Aristotle in theology, with such unhappy results! Yet twelve centuries later the Church was moved by God to do the very same thing, and to the great advantage of Catholics. Sabellius tried to clarify the numerical oneness of Divinity, only to fall into heresy. It took time for Catholics to discover the right way of presenting that most sacred dogma. Finally Augustine, doctor of the Church, fully expounded the dogma; the creed *Quicumque* confirmed it; the fourth Lateran Council defined it. The Montanists affected prophecy, and what was that but a presumptuous anticipation of teachers of the Church. The religious constituted a certain order, with a Benedict or a Francis as a kind of hierarch. They teach the development of discipline, if not of dogmas. They insist on the infallibility of the judge divinely appointed in matters of faith. But Montanus was his own judge in such matters, not the Catholic Church.

Perrone's Notes on Thesis Twelve

(1) My comments can be summarized by the following propositions: First, the Church was always conscious of all the truths

of faith divinely entrusted to her. Second, this deposit was entrusted whole and entire to that same Church. Third, truths of faith are not in themselves capable of growth, but only of being expounded more explicitly. Fourth, as a result, those truths do not grow materially, to use the scholastic expression, or in themselves, but only in relation to our greater awareness or more distinct knowledge of them by means of ecclesiastical definition, not, as they say, with respect to them, but only with respect to us.

Appendix One

Perrone's 1867 Letter to Newman

Very Reverend Father Newman,

Supposing Your Reverence has not altogether forgotten our lovely Italian language, I send you a few lines in that idiom.

I am grateful, first of all, that your kind remembrance of me has lasted. You could scarcely believe how very much I have always liked and admired Your Reverence. Whenever I think of you I draw consolation from the good you have achieved, and are still accomplishing, for that England of yours. That achievement will not rise to heaven unattended, but with a fine crown and halo from you and your Oratory, and drawn by the souls your ministry has brought out of their darkness, into the light of the holy and apostolic Church of Rome. I pray God may never cease to bless your zeal and your labors for a more abounding harvest.

I am aware that in recent times Your Reverence has experienced bitter disappointments, and I have felt them as though they were my own. But I do not think God can have failed to compensate by his grace, bringing you consolation and encouragement, as he does with souls he cherishes. You know that God purifies us by means of afflictions, and makes us less unworthy of him. The life of his divine Son on this earth was one of constant suffering, a cross from start to finish, and such must be the lives of those who love him and serve him faithfully. May patience and forbearance accompany you on this brief pilgrimage.

In the end your true homeland will embrace you with unending joy.

Occasions have arisen on which I have undertaken your defense, and done so with good success. From the nature of the case, I am unable to say more about that. But should another occasion present itself, have no doubt that you will find me always ready to defend your cause. Throughout our lives there are always adversaries. The Lord makes use of them to test our fidelity and perseverance. But in the end, God will see to it that victory goes to truth and innocence.

My unworthiness diminishes the value of my prayers. But, such as they are, I shall not fail to offer them to God in your behalf. And I hope Your Reverence will not fail to do the same for me. My heart remains always united with yours in Jesus Christ, our love and our hope. Be of good courage. Trust in God. He will be with you.

It has been a joy for me to be able with these few lines to converse in confidence with one whom I value so highly. With feelings of sincere attachment to Your Reverence, I am

Humbly, devotedly, respectfully,

Giovanni Perrone, S.J.

Appendix Two

Most dear and Reverend Father Giovanni Perrone, S.J.,

The letter I received from you yesterday, dear Reverend Father, has filled me with joy and with the tenderest gratitude. Who am I, that after so many years I still find a place in your memory and in your heart? And how have I deserved your vindicating and defending me with such charity?

Your defending me is no less an honor than it is a help. I shall never be troubled by the caprices of the immature and impetuous as long as I have not wholly displeased so seasoned and solid a scholar as your Reverence. That is also greatly reassuring to me. For although well aware that I am no theologian, I have tried my best in some of my books to treat certain theological matters with care and accuracy. It is most gratifying to understand that I have written about these matters in a way that satisfies not only me, but also you.

In your charity, do keep me in your prayers, most Reverend Father.

With great respect and love,

John Henry Newman

from our Oratory
5th May 1867

Newman's 1877 Preface to
The Via Media of the Anglican Church

Introduction

Newman's 1847 summary in Latin of his views on the development of doctrine was deferential almost to a fault. His main concern was simply to obtain an unbiased hearing from theologically competent Catholic critics of a theory that had contributed greatly to his own decision to enter the Roman Catholic Church. He was still in many ways a stranger to the culture of that church, and especially naive about its current political complexion. He had already been made wary by opposition that appeared to be neither forthright nor informed.

Father Perrone's cooperation had proved encouraging, and his apparent comfort with Newman's ideas about development was reassuring. In the years that followed, Newman's *Essay on the Development of Christian Doctrine* gained many admirers. It continued, however, to be widely distrusted in the most conservative circles of the Catholic Church, and during most of Newman's life those circles included the pope and the principal Catholic hierarchy in England. Newman did not again write directly on this topic nor did he publish in any form the document he had shared with Perrone. It is clear, however, that his views about the topic persisted, and that his conviction of its importance remained strong. He did come close to one aspect of the topic in 1859, when he wrote in the *Rambler* about consulting the faithful in matters of doctrine. This piece generated a furor that absolutely astonished its author and drove him into semi-seclusion for some time afterwards. He was removed from his editorship, chided by his ecclesiastical superiors, and even denounced to Rome as heretical, all for seeming to suggest that there was good patristic precedent for considering the views of laypeople when formulating church teachings.

Another aspect of doctrinal development became the center of public and even political controversy in England following the first Vatican Council's dogmatic definition of papal infallibility in 1870. In this instance it was recognized that, distrusted though he was by Catholic hierarchy, Newman was the only English Catholic who could respond effectively to Anglican critics who included even the Prime Minister. Newman accepted the task, but defended the doctrine of papal infallibility interpreted much more moderately than it was by the conservative hierarchy. This defense of a .Catholic doctrine cherished by conservative extremists thus carried with it an implicit rejection of their extremism. Newman was as Catholic as he had ever been, but shrewder than he had once been in dealing with partisan churchmanship, and less deferential to views that he had come to perceive as fanatical.

It was seven years later that Newman returned spontaneously and directly to the matter of doctrinal development. He did so first of all by publishing a new edition of the *Essay on the Development of Christian Doctrine,* incorporating some reorganization of the material and some alterations "not indeed in its matter, but in its text." This latter phrase from the preface to the new edition indicates that for Newman himself, the book had stood the test of time and criticism. And in republishing it after twenty years as a Roman Catholic he implicitly affirmed its orthodoxy and its continuing usefulness to inquirers.

What may be more remarkable than his decision to republish the book that had ushered him into the Roman Catholic Church was his deciding in the same year to issue a new edition of the earlier book which argued for his remaining in the Church of England, namely the two volumes of his *Via Media*. This was the book that defended a theory in which Newman had been unable to maintain confidence. As he himself had observed, "I found the *Via Media* less and less satisfactory. It broke down with me in 1839." Why, then, republish as a Roman Catholic a work severely critical of Roman Catholicism and which the author himself had regarded as unsatisfactory for nearly forty years? Newman gives as his main reason an apprehension that, after his death, the book might be used in support of Anglicanism and against the Roman Catholic Church. To prevent that, he proposed to republish it, unaltered, but accompanied by additional material explaining his subsequent rejection of its argument and his misgivings about some specific contents. There is, however, more to it than that.

Newman did not consider the *Via Media* simply as an old bomb that needed to be defused now that he had gone over to the other side. In rejecting its argument he had not rejected wholesale the material he had assembled to support the argument. As he now explains, in a preface to the new edition, controversial writings have three typical components. They present in the first place "truths and facts, together with deductions from them." They also contain "hypothesis, as a substitute for direct evidence." And the third, less respectable content, is "coarse rhetoric of hard names and sweeping imputations in advance of proof." Looking back now, with his Roman Catholic convictions, at the *Via Media*, Newman was eager to disown both his harsh words about the Church of Rome, and hypotheses afterwards tested and found untenable.

Newman's rejection of the theory of the *Via Media* was based on new arguments that mainly comprise his *Essay on the Development of Christian Doctrine,* about to be republished. But there was another issue raised by the *Via Media* which, Newman reflected, "I have nowhere treated from a Roman Catholic point of view; yet it certainly has a claim to be explained; and . . . at least I can show how I explain it to myself." This other issue about the Roman Catholic Church, "which is equally obvious and equally serious, is the difference which at first sight presents itself between its formal teaching and its popular and political manifestations." Newman had made a satisfactory case for Roman Catholicism's defined dogmas as authentic doctrinal developments, that is, as elements of the original revelation which, in the course of time and under the influence of controversy, were made explicit articles of belief. But that left unaccounted for a great many aspects of Catholic popular belief and piety, of pastoral preaching, of church discipline, practice and policy, and of teachings having no strict claim to infallibility. Most of what Newman had cited in the *Via Media* as casting doubt on the claims of Roman Catholicism was not strict dogmatic definitions, but came from this larger body of beliefs, doctrines, and practices. And in looking back at the instances he had cited of this problematic material, Newman did not find himself generally mistaken about the facts. The history of Roman Catholicism was an extremely untidy history, strewn with improprieties and inconsistencies. Yet there was, for Newman, nothing astonishing about that. As he had said in the *Via Media,* "the whole course of Christianity from the first, when we come to examine it, is but one series of troubles and disorders." It was that way before the Reformation as well as after; it could hardly be otherwise in the Roman Catholic Church. Such was the case. But, Newman now asked, why was it the case? Why did not the history of genuine Christianity, founded by Christ, guided by the Spirit, and protected from fundamental error, display a calm, smooth, harmonious course? Newman's interest in that question can hardly have been purely academic. His own personal experience of twenty years in the Church he regarded as the true Church of Christ had been anything but serene. He had observed innumerable consequences of ignorant and irresponsible conduct of the Church's affairs by its official pastors. He had experienced enough unfairness and insensitivity from the leaders of the Church to have no doubt that such abuses were commonplace and their motives widespread. The long history he had studied and the short history he had experienced were unanimous in their testimony to the Church's chronic turbulence and its incompetence in dealing with it. Neither the long history nor the short one had shaken his faith in the Church's authenticity. But they had caused him to wonder and, eventually, to offer an explanation. It is that explanation, a highly original one, that Newman elaborated in his new preface to the 1877 re-edition of the *Via Media*. Although commonly recognized by those who have read it, especially in recent times, as a valuable and useful resource for theologians, its circulation has not been facilitated by its location in an early, little-read, and usually out-of-print work of which Newman himself had rejected the main argument. Hence its inclusion in this presentation of Newman's relatively inaccessible Roman Catholic writings on development.

Newman's basic answer to his basic question, of why there is so much chaos in the Church's history, is simple and commonsensical. It is because the Church undertakes to do too many things at once, or, more precisely, too many kinds of things at once. But in describing the problem in this way Newman does not envisage any solution to it. The several kinds of things the Church tries to do simultaneously are not optional. They are part of the Church's very definition. Yet they are kinds of things that inevitably pull sometimes in different directions and have disorderly outcomes. Such situations occur often in human life. Legitimate interests conflict. Conscientious practices collide. Demands of duty diverge. Newman recalls familiar instances of "how difficult it is for one and the same man to satisfy independent duties and incommensurable relations; to act at once as a parent and a judge, as a soldier and minister of religion, as a philosopher and a statesman, as a courtier or a politician and a Catholic; the rules of conduct in these various positions being so distinct, and the obligations so contrary." The Church has, and cannot relinquish similarly contrasting and conflictual roles. What it does in one sphere may, in its effect on other spheres, seem overdone or underdone, exaggerated or slighted. This becomes evident the moment one considers what are the Church's defining roles, offices, or functions. According to tradition, the Church has three such roles, derived from and reflecting Christ. As Christ is said to be Prophet, Priest, and King, so the Church is called upon to teach, sanctify and rule. It must, by divine mandate, proclaim revealed truth, preside over religious worship, and maintain ecclesiastical discipline. And doing equal justice to all three functions is often difficult.   The kind of difficulty Newman envisages is, as his examples suggest, quite familiar to most people. Thus, the mothers and fathers of children are normally inclined and generally expected to be for their children at once a friend, teacher, and disciplinarian, and to be all these in a very special way. But every mother or father who has ever tried to do this has experienced how often each step forward in one of these functions seems to foster retrogression in the others. Good parents do not despair, but they do resign themselves to imperfect achievements and watch themselves lest one of their roles so predominate that the others are seriously neglected. And wise parents know that their own personalities and current circumstances encourage certain biases that can easily get out of hand. An absolutely perfect parent could, presumably, maintain a flawless balance among these different functions. But such parents do not exist. The same might be expected of a flawless church, but that does not exist either. Nor is the problem solved for the church by infallibility. As Newman put it, "nothing but the gift of impeccability granted to her authorities" could ensure that her functions remained in perfect balance, "and such a gift they have not received." Being protected against dogmatic corruption is one thing. It is quite another thing to be exempted from the foibles and partialities, the knavery and folly, of common humanity. That the Roman Catholic Church's authorities had not been favored with any such exemption was something of which Newman had had many painful reminders.

Over the broad span of church history, instances could be found of any one of the church's functions working against the others. An obsessively theological church easily loses the fervor of piety. Excesses on the devotional side tempt theology to rationalize superstitions. Exaggerated preoccupation with discipline generates repression of freedom both of thought and of spirituality. All of these things had happened, again and again, in the history of Roman Catholicism. In Newman's view this was, broadly speaking, simply inevitable. "Is it not plain," he asked, "that if one determinate course is to be taken by the Church, acting at once in all three capacities, so opposed to each other in their idea, that course must, as I have said, be deflected from the line which would be traced out by any one of them if viewed by itself, or else the requirements of one or two sacrificed to the interests of the third."

Although Newman's theory is presented mainly as a key to interpreting persistently erratic features of Catholic Church teaching, it is clearly applicable not only to understanding the Church's past behavior, but also to criticizing it in present circumstances. The basic procedure is to ask, whenever Church decisions appear unbalanced or eccentric, if the circumstances do not suggest a conflict among the Prophetic, Priestly, and Kingly offices. If such seems to be the case, the next step is to observe which of those offices was allowed to predominate over the others. And the final step is to decide whether, in the circumstances, that predominance was justified.

Although any of the three offices can preponderate, during Newman's lifetime it was always the same one. For Pius IX the Kingly office was notoriously hyperactive, while theology was stultified and worship narrowly confined. Newman had experienced the sheer dullness of thought from his first months in the Roman Catholic Church. But, worse than dullness he had experienced a morbid atmosphere of suspicion and censoriousness that habitually shunned candid discussion and easily lapsed into defamatory gossip. That authoritarian government in the Church was subject to the vices of secular politics Newman had no doubt. The new edition of the *Via Media* reaffirmed what he had said while still an Anglican, "There may indeed be holiness in the religious aspect of the Church, and soundness in her theological, but still there is in her the ambition, craft and cruelty of a political power."

Newman's theory of conflict among the Church's defining offices is essentially a diagnostic instrument. The condition it serves to diagnose is not, in Newman's view, strictly curable. But it can be modified and kept within reasonable bounds if it is clearly understood, and Newman's theory is a help towards understanding it.

Preface to the Third Edition of the *Via Media*

I propose here in some introductory pages to consider, first, how far and with what argumentative force these Lectures, published just forty years since, bear upon the teaching in faith and morals of the Catholic Church, against which they were more or less directed; and next what satisfactory answer can be given in explanation of the main charges in which they issue. As to incidental objections and matters of detail, they shall be dealt with in bracketed notes, *in loco,* at the foot of the page, as they occur.*

Part I.

1

I have said that these Lectures are "more or less" directed against points in Catholic teaching, and that I should consider "how far," because it must be borne in mind that the formal purpose of the Volume was, not an attack upon that teaching, but the establishment of a doctrine of its own, the Anglican *Via Media.* It only indirectly comes into collision with the theology of Rome. That theology lay in the very threshold of the author's experiment; he came across it, whether he would or no, and, while he attacked

---

*In this edition of the Preface, Newman's footnotes are presented as endnotes on pages 125-126.

it at considerable length in its details, he adopted its main principles and many of its conclusions; and, as obliterating thereby or ignoring the very rudiments of Protestantism, he acted far more as an assailant of the religion of the Reformation than of what he called "Popery."

"The immediate reason," he says in his Introduction, "for discussing the subject [of the Church] is this: In the present day such incidental notice of it, as Christian teachers are led to take in the course of their pastoral instructions, is sure to be charged with what is commonly called 'Popery:' and for this reason – that, Romanists having ever insisted upon it, and Protestants having neglected it, to speak of it at all, though it is mentioned in the Creed, is thought to savour of Romanism. Those then who feel its importance, and yet are not Romanists, are bound on several accounts to show why they are not Romanists, and how they differ from them." (*infr.,* p. 5)[†]

He continues: "This happens for another reason. After all, the main subject in discussion should be, not to refute error merely, but to establish truth. . . [Christians] have a demand on their teachers for the meaning of the article of the Creed, which binds them to faith 'in the Holy Catholic Church.' . . . To do this effectually, we must proceed on the plan of attacking Romanism, as the most convenient method of exhibiting our own views about it. It has preoccupied the ground, and we cannot erect our own structure without partly breaking down, partly using what we find upon it. And thus for a second reason the following Lectures, as far as their very form goes, are chiefly written against Romanism, though their main object is not controversy, but edification," pp. 6, 7.

Nay, still further, as a matter of duty, he made it a special point in the composition of his Volume to inflict

---

[†]Newman's page references are to the first volume of the third edition of his *Via Media.*

upon his own people the intellectual force, nay the truth of the Roman teaching, viewed as a whole, in spite of large and serious errors in detail, in order to open Protestant eyes to the weakness of Protestant polemics, and to persuade Protestant divines to fall back and take up a safer position, giving up what they could not hope to retain, and maintaining by sound and clear argument what they could not religiously surrender. Hence, large portions of these Lectures are expositions, nay, recommendations of principles and doctrines, recognized in the Catholic Church, and in these portions, now that I take up the Volume afresh as a Catholic, I have nothing or little to alter.

2

Such is a good part of the first Lecture, which is on the subject of Tradition, and explains and professes Catholic teaching respecting it with very few statements which require correction or addition. The doctrine treated in the second Lecture is that of the cogency of Ancient Consent or of the testimony of Antiquity; and here again what Catholics hold is accurately expounded and affirmed, though at the same time various instances are adduced to show that Catholics in practice contradict the principle which they formally profess.

The third and fourth Lectures are anti-catholic from beginning to end, and constitute the special portion of the Volume which is antagonistic to the Roman Church. These two Lectures are mainly occupied in tracing the supposed evils which come of the doctrine of Infallibility, though in a later Lecture the author seems to consider that privilege as having been intended by Divine Providence for His Church, and as actually enjoyed by her for some centuries.

The fifth, on Private Judgment, is a delineation and defense of the *Via Media,* for which on the whole it is little more than an apology, confessing it to be, as a doctrine, wanting in simplicity, hard to master, indeterminate in its provisions, and without a substantive existence in any age or country.

The sixth, which is on the abuse of Private Judgment, might have been written by a Catholic, and so might the first part of the seventh, till the argument passes on to an attack upon the doctrines of Purgatory and Papal Supremacy.

In the eighth, ninth, and tenth, amid much which a Catholic would condemn and protest against, it is allowed that the Church, which the Apostles founded, is "ever divinely guided to teach the truth," is "indefectible in her witness of the Christian faith," "has a supernatural gift" for the purpose of transmitting it, and is "unerring, infallible, in matters of saving faith."

The three which follow, the eleventh, twelfth, and thirteenth, on Scripture as the Rule of Faith, are in such wise guarded and explained as virtually to admit, while denying, the authority of Tradition, and are for the most part in accordance, or reconcilable, with Catholic belief on the subject, in spite of some misconception of our teaching, and of language which needs correction.

The last Lecture, like the Introduction, is a candid confession of the shortcomings and reverses of the Anglican Establishment, and only so far injurious to the Catholic Church as it is an attempt to shelter such misfortunes, past or present, behind those scandals, of which the Church herself has been from time to time the victim.

Thus at least one half of the Volume, as I consider, is taken up with an advocacy, unexceptionable more or less, of Catholic principles and doctrines; with this I can have no quarrel, and must turn to the other half, if I am to find matter for it. Such matter no doubt there is, and serious too; but, before proceeding to it, I have to distinguish between those statements or charges which can claim an answer, as being argumentative, and those which cannot.

3

I observe then that controversial writings are for the most part made up of three main elements, only one of which is, strictly speaking, of an argumentative character, meaning by argument truths and facts, together with deductions from them. This last is the logical element; but there are other two instruments in controversy seldom dispensed with by those who engage in it, and more or less rhetorical, and which, though they may have a considerable place in these Lectures, have no claim to a place in this Preface.

One of these two is the free use of hypothesis, as a substitute for direct evidence and hard reasoning, in support of propositions which have to be maintained; I mean, a suggestion of views more or less probable or possible, and either consistent, or not inconsistent, or perhaps in actual concurrence, as ideas, with the facts of the case; and this, in order to reconcile difficulties and answer objections, to supplement what is obscure or deficient, to bring together into one separate matters which seem to be without a meaning, and to assign a law for them, where none was suspected.

Such hypotheses are altogether legitimate, and often necessary; for representations may be true, which nevertheless are not or cannot be proved; and probabilities, when accumulated, tell, and new openings for thought and for discovery are sometimes the issue of what is in the first instance little more than a conjecture. Still such hypotheses appeal to the imagination more than to the reasoning faculty; and, while by their plausibility, ingenuity, or brilliancy, they may gain from the reader more sympathy than is strictly their due, they do not admit, and on that account cannot demand, a logical refutation. Reason cannot be called on to demolish what reason has not even professed to establish.

For instance, in answer to the argument against the Plurality of Worlds, drawn from the fact that first presents itself to scientific observation on the question, viz. that the Moon is but a cinder unsuitable to animal life, it has been objected, I believe, that, for what we know, a rich soil, a profuse vegetation, and races of animals, sentient and intellectual, may be on the hemisphere, which we never see. This is an hypothesis for the occasion; and till arguments are adduced in its behalf, it cannot challenge a reply. So also, it is an hypothesis to suggest, with a view to reconcile the Scripture text about the creation of Adam with recent scientific possibilities as to the origin and past duration of man, that the second chapter of Genesis and the first relate to different creations, and that there was a race of pre-Adamites.

4

Such is an hypothesis; and, to come to the subject of these Lectures, such also is the Via Media, a possible road, lying between a mountain and a morass, to be driven through formidable obstacles, if it is to exist, by the boldness and skill of the engineers. It is projected and planned for a definite necessity, the necessity of the Anglican position, except for which it would never have been imagined; and, as many other projects and plans, it may be made to look very fair on paper. And this dressing up of an hypothesis being the scope of the Author's undertaking here, it is not wonderful, that he should be all through *"qualis ab incepto;"* that he should be fertile in hypotheses in subservience to his main theory, as expedients for successive emergencies, that he should aim at consistency in his statements rather than at proof founded on evidence, and in consequence that, for the most part, he cannot claim to be formally refuted.

And, indeed, he starts with a profession which, unobjectionable as it is in itself, prepares the reader for the unsubstantial character of the discussions which are to follow. "What Christians especially need and have a right to expect," he says in the Introduction, "is a *positive doctrine* on such subjects as come under notice. . . . It is a poor answer merely to set about an attack upon Romanism. . . . Erroneous or not, a view it certainly does contain, and that religion, which attempts a view, though imperfect or extreme, does more than those who do not attempt it at all," p. 6. I subscribe to this doctrine as reasonable and true; but, as to its bearing on the Author's undertaking, two things were necessary for the defense of the Anglican Church, a broad, intellectual, intelligible theory, and a logical and historical foundation for that theory; and he was content to attempt the former, taking the latter for granted.

Proof was not the main object of his book; as far as he aimed at proof in behalf of Anglicanism, he insisted on its reasonableness and consistency: and this, though at the same time he was accusing the theology of Rome of basing itself on consistency to the neglect of truth. He avows that Christianity itself does not in the first place depend on or require argument. He thinks the very preaching of it sufficient to secure its victory. "Truth," he says, "has the gift of overcoming the human heart, whether by persuasion or compulsion; and, if what we preach be truth, it must be natural, it must be popular, it will make itself popular," p. 15. Here again I go with him: I readily grant in particular that there is much truth in Anglican teaching, and that, so far, it does and will, while it lasts, powerfully affect the multitude of men, to whom it comes; but I cannot allow to the Church of England itself what is true of much of its teaching and many of its teachers, for that teaching and those teachers, who are so effective, know nothing of the *Via Media.*

However, this innate persuasiveness, as he considered it, of the *Via Media,* was in truth the writer's chief stay in the controversy. He did not set much by patristical literature or by history. He frankly allows that his theory had never been realized, and that for 1800 years the true Gospel, as regards his special aspect of it, had never been preached to the world. "The doctrines in question," he says, in the mouth of an objector, "are in one sense as entirely new, as Christianity was when first preached. Protestantism and Popery are real religions . . . they have furnished the mould in which nations have been cast; but the *Via Media,* viewed as an integral system, has scarcely had existence, except on paper." He adds, "It cannot be denied there is force in these representations, though I would not adopt them to their full extent," pp. 16, 17.

As to the ante-Nicene period, made so much of by Anglican divines, he limits himself to the task of ascertaining "what is the *nearest approximation* to that primitive truth which Ignatius and Polycarp enjoyed, and which the 19th century has virtually lost?" p. 7. It was almost enough for him that the Fathers did not contradict him, and that he was not obliged absolutely to part company with them; for, as matters stood, he felt the Anglican hypothesis could shoot up and thrive in the gaps between the trees which were the pride of the Eden of primitive truth, neither choking nor choked by their foliage. And he hoped to be able to retain Origen and Cyprian, though he held by Laud.

5

So much in the Introduction and the Lectures which follow are in keeping with it. Take, for instance, the fifth, on Private Judgment, it is scarcely more than a gratuitous hypothesis from beginning to end, supported neither by Scripture, nor Antiquity – and an intricate hypothesis, as the Author confesses. "It cannot easily be mastered," he says, "first, because it is of a complex nature, involving a combination of principles, and depending on multiplied conditions; next, because it partakes of that indeterminateness, which is to a certain extent the characteristic of English theology; lastly, because it has never been realized," p. 129. Accordingly he "attempts to *describe* it, first in theory, and then *as if* reduced to practice." To prove it from the Fathers, or from the nature of the case, does not enter into the scope of his undertaking. When he has finished his sketch of it, he assures the reader that *"he really does believe,"* p. 143, that in point of "primitive simplicity, rational freedom, truth and certainty," his rule of determining revealed doctrine is better than the Roman.

And so, when he comes to the question of the indefectibility of the Church, though he argues, and plausibly, from the parallel of the Jewish dispensation, that gifts may have been intended for an elect people, and even promised them, of which they came short in the event, yet he is far more bent on distinguishing between the Roman and the Anglican teaching on the subject under review, than on proving the Anglican to be true. He says, "I have said enough by way of distinguishing between our own and the Roman theology, and of showing that neither our concessions are reluctantly made, nor our differences subtle and nugatory, as is objected by opponents," p. 211. And further on: "These distinctions are surely portions of a real view, which, while it relieves the mind of those burdens and perplexities which are the portion of the mere Protestant, is essentially distinct from Romanism," p. 213. To draw out these distinctions, indeed, was his primary reason for writing about the Roman Church at all, as he stated in a passage already quoted.

6

So much on one of the non-logical aspects, under which these Lectures may in their controversial character be regarded. The other, though often presented to us in such works, is not so blameless. It is the coarse rhetoric of hard names and sweeping imputations in advance of proof, proof not only not adduced, but not even promised. In controversy one has no right to complain of strong conclusions, but to assume them on starting is the act of a pleader or advocate, not of a theologian. I will not indeed say that this aim in polemical attack is altogether inadmissible, but at least it is not logical, and may without scruple be ignored and passed over by a respondent. It is at times, and in a measure pardonable, when it stands for a token or symbol of earnestness in an assailant, and of confidence in the goodness of his cause. From the freshness and originality of thought which gives life to such rhetoric – or from the authority of the speaker or writer which gives it weight – or from the congeniality of strong words in the matter in dispute with the sentiments of the audience or hearer – or from their terseness and keenness as *dicta,* appeals, denunciations, defiances – or again as the vehicle of humorous images, satirical nick-names, epigrammatic hits – or as watchwords in a great conflict – they may be serviceable, nay, indispensable, in exciting attention and interest, in encouraging the wavering or timid, and in diffusing light over subjects obscure or abstruse; but after all, or for the most part, their proper place is public meetings or the Courts of Law, and, when disjoined from argument, they are as unworthy of ecclesiastics as they are easy and seductive.

7

I wish these Lectures did not furnish instances of this reprehensible polemic. There was a great deal of calling of names all through them (I do not mean as regards individuals but as against "Romanism"), of which the Author has cause to be ashamed. That very word "Romanism," together with "Romanist" and "Romish," is an instance, though not the worst. It is not the worst, first from the great need there is of some word to take its place in the case of an Anglican controversialist, who could not consistently with his own pretensions use the right words Catholic and Catholicity. And again the offensive word had a specific and definite meaning, convenient in polemical writings, even if elsewhere improper. It was not used in this Volume simply for Catholics and their religion; but for that particular aspect, which both their faith and they themselves bore, when they identified themselves with the See of Rome and its characteristic claims and tenets.[1] The more a writer revered that wonderful See and followed its teaching and, several years before these Lectures appeared, their Author had spoken of "the high gifts and strong claims of the Church of Rome on our admiration, reverence, love, and gratitude," and had asked how we could "refrain from melting into tenderness and rushing into communion with it," but for its errors), the more he had these feelings towards it, the more he needed a word which would distinguish what he accepted from what scandalized him. One of the characteristics of this Volume, of which I shall have to say much presently, is the recurring contrast insisted on in it between the theological side of Roman teaching and its political and popular side; and it was the latter which the Author had chiefly in mind when he spoke of Romanists and Romanism. However, Catholics feel that appellation to be a nick-name, whatever may be said in its defense; and it does not become those who are so sensitive at being called Protestants (though Laud took the title to himself on the scaffold), to inflict on us an ambiguous designation which we refuse to accept.

8

Worse than the use of this word are the vague charges, and random reproaches, and scornful epithets indulged in by the Author, keenly alive as he was to the vulgarity of the Exeter Hall eloquence of the day. Thus we are told of "the bold speculativeness of "Romanism," "the bold exactness of Romanism," "the presumptuous dogmatism of Rome," "the reckless conduct of Rome," and of "that venturesome Church." We are told that, "Rome would classify and number all things and settle every question;" that this is its "pernicious," its "mischievous peculiarity;" that Roman Divines are "ever intruding into things not seen as yet;" that they "venture to touch the ark," and "give an opening to pride and self-confidence;" that "in Romanism there would seem to be little room for unconscious devotion;" that it is especially "characteristic of Romanism to indulge the carnal tastes of the multitude;" that it is "shallow as a philosophy, and dangerous to the Christian spirit;" that "if earth is the standard and heaven the instrument, Rome is most happy in her religious system;" that she is "bent on proselytizing, organizing and ruling, as the end of life;" that her doctrine of infallibility is "an effort, presumptuous and unwarranted, as well as founded in error, to stem the tide of unbelief;" that "Romanism makes the Church the instrument of a double usurpation," and as to Roman Divines, "as in the building of Babel, God has confounded their language."

Sometimes the offense is greater still, because the Author goes out of his way to aim a side-blow at Rome, or, again, by some violent words against her to cover some quasi-Catholic statement, which was likely to be unpalatable to his readers: thus, after saying that the treatment by Petavius of the early Fathers is parricide, which he had a right to say, if he so felt, he will not admit that it was an extreme case without the ungracious circumlocution, "Rome even, steeled as she is against the kindlier feelings, when her interests require, has more of tender-mercy left than to bear this often." And elsewhere, after saying that "the Romanists have no difficulty in answering" a particular "question," he gratuitously adds, "unscrupulousness commonly makes a clear way."

The most serious of these passages is that at the commencement of the third Lecture, in which derangement or a worse calamity is attributed to the Roman Church. This passage I included in the list of Retractations which I published several years before I became a Catholic, and, as it will be printed at the end of the second of these Volumes which I am editing, I have omitted a portion of it in its proper place; and, together with it, other phrases and sentences which occur here and there; that is, such as were not necessary for the logical continuity, or the explicitness or the force of the context in which they occur.

9

Putting aside, then, what I have called the rhetorical elements of the Lectures under review, I come now in the third place to that portion of them which may be considered argumentative. This is mainly to be found in the Second, Third, and Fourth, which severally survey the Church of Rome in her patristical, moral, and political aspects. And I shall have no difficulty in admitting on the whole the definite facts and statements which are there made the ground of charges against Catholic teaching. Those alleged facts and statements were the result of a careful and not unfriendly study of Bellarmine's great work, and are in substance accurate. Of the charges themselves, however, I cannot speak so favourably; they are for the most part made at second hand; but, since the Author took upon himself the responsibility, they ought to have been the issue of his own independent judgment, not the opinions of Laud, Taylor, or Leslie. They are portions for the most part of that *Via Media* teaching, which is characteristic of the divines of the Anglican School. He admitted far too easily what those divines said about the early Fathers, and what they said about Rome, the chief work he took upon himself being that of systematizing what they had variously put forth.

This indeed he professes to be his special aim in the Introduction to these Lectures. "It is proposed," he says, "to offer helps towards the formation of a recognized; Anglican theology in one of its departments. The most vigorous, the clearest, the most fertile minds have been employed in the service of our Church, minds too as reverential and holy, and as fully imbued with Ancient Truth, and as well versed in the writings of the Fathers, as they were intellectually gifted. One thing is still wanting: we have a vast inheritance, but no inventory of our treasures. All is given us in profusion; it remains for us to catalogue, sort, distribute, select, harmonize, and complete," p. 24 and so on.

In the years which followed the publication of this Volume, in proportion as he read the Fathers more carefully, and used his own eyes in determining the faith and worship of their times, his confidence in the Anglican divines was more and more shaken, and at last it went altogether. And, according as this change of mind came over him, he felt of course disturbance at that strong language he had used against the Roman teaching, on which I have animadverted above, and which, though he had used it with a full belief that it was merited and was necessary for the Anglican argument, had never been quite according to his taste. At length he published a Retractation of the chief passages which were coloured with it. And he felt no thanks at all to the writers in whom he had so rashly confided. In the words of the *Apologia pro Vitâ Suâ* –

> Not only did I think such language necessary for my Church's religious position, but I recollected that all the great Anglican divines had thought so before me. They had thought so, and they had acted accordingly. . . . We all know the story of the convict, who on the scaffold bit off his mother's ear. . . . I was in a humour certainly to bite off their ears. . . . I thought they had taken me in. I had read the Fathers with their eyes, I had sometimes trusted their quotations or their reasonings. . . . I had thought myself safe, while I had their warrant for what I said. I had exercised more faith than criticism in the matter. This did not imply any broad misstatements on my part, arising from reliance on their authority, but it implied carelessness in matters of detail, and this of course was a fault."

10

However, in thus speaking of the polemical statements which I rashly made my own, I do not mean that nothing at once plausible and important has been brought by the Anglican writers against the doctrine, worship, organization, government, and historical action of the Catholic Church. They have in fact made several broad charges, which cannot be shuffled away, but demand a formal and careful answer. Some of these charges were reproduced in these Lectures, two of them of special importance. Of these, one I have considered in a former publication, and the other shall be the subject of the pages which follow.

I address myself to this latter objection in particular, because I have made it on many occasions and in many ways. I am not undertaking here to defend the Catholic Church against all assailants whatever, but against one, that is, myself. I say this lest readers should consider I have done nothing unless I refute such allegations as these – that Rome dwarfs the intellect, narrows the mind, hardens the heart, fosters superstition, and encourages a blood-thirsty, crafty, and bigoted temper – these are charges which this Volume does not contain.

Part II

1

I am not here addressing those who unhappily find themselves unable to profess Christianity. I shall assume a great number of principles and facts, which they will deny; as they on their part often cause me to wonder and grieve, by the strange assumptions they themselves make without hesitation or remorse. But there are those, not a few, who would be Catholics, if their conscience would let them; for they see in the Catholic Religion a great substance and earnest of truth; a depth, strength, coherence, elasticity, and life, a nobleness and grandeur, a power of sympathy and resource in view of the various ailments of the soul, and a suitableness to all classes and circumstances of mankind; a glorious history, and a promise of perpetual youthfulness; and they already accept without scruple or rather joyfully feed upon its solemn mysteries, which are a trial to others; but they cannot, as a matter of duty, enter its fold on account of certain great difficulties which block their way, and throw them back, when they would embrace that faith which looks so like what it professes to be.

To these I would address myself, as far as my discussion on a very large subject extends; and, even if I do not succeed with them, at least I shall be explaining, as I have long wished to do, how I myself get over difficulties which I formerly felt as well as they, and which made me for many years cry out bitterly, "Union with Rome is impossible." Most probably I shall be able to do little more. It is so ordered on high that in our day Holy Church should present just that aspect to my countrymen which is most consonant with their ingrained prejudices against her, most unpromising for their conversion; and what can one writer do to counteract this misfortune? But enough of this; whatever comes of it, I must be content to have done what I feel it an obligation to do.

2

Two broad charges are brought against the Catholic Religion in these Lectures, and in some of the tracts and other Papers that follow. One is the contrast which modern Catholicism is said to present with the religion of the Primitive Church, in teaching, conduct, worship, and polity, and this difficulty I have employed myself in discussing and explaining at great length in my Essay on Development of Doctrine, published in 1845.

The other, which is equally obvious and equally serious, is the difference which at first sight presents itself between its formal teaching and its popular and political manifestations; for instance, between the teaching of the Breviary and of the Roman Catechism on the one hand, and the spirit and tone of various manuals of Prayer and Meditation and of the Sermons or Addresses of ecclesiastics in high position on the other. This alleged discordance I have nowhere treated from a Catholic point of view; yet it certainly has a claim to be explained; and, as

I have said, at least I can show how I explain it to myself, even though others refuse to take my explanation.

3

My answer shall be this: that from the nature of the case, such an apparent contrariety between word and deed, the abstract and the concrete, could not but take place, supposing the Church to be gifted with those various prerogatives, and charged with those independent and conflicting duties, which Anglicans, as well as ourselves, recognize as belonging to her. Her organization cannot be otherwise than complex, considering the many functions which she has to fulfill, the many aims to keep in view, the many interests to secure – functions, aims, and interests, which in their union and divergence remind us of the prophet's vision of the Cherubim, in whom "the wings of one were joined to the wings of another," yet "they turned not, when they went, but every one went straight forward." Or, to speak without figure, we know in matters of this world, how difficult it is for one and the same man to satisfy independent duties and incommensurable relations; to act at once as a parent and a judge, as a soldier and a minister of religion, as a philosopher and a statesman, as a courtier or a politician and a Catholic; the rules of conduct in these various positions being so distinct, and the obligations so contrary. Prudent men keep clear, if they can, of such perplexities; but as to the Church, gifted as she is with grace up to the measure of her responsibilities, if she has on her an arduous work, it is sufficient to refer to our Lord's words, "What is impossible with men, is possible with God," in order to be certain (in spite of appearances) of her historical uprightness and consistency. At the same time it may undeniably have happened before now that her rulers and authorities, as men, on certain occasions have come short of what was required of them, and have given occasion to criticism, just or unjust, on account of the special antagonisms or compromises by means of which her many-sided mission under their guidance has been carried out.

4

With this introduction 1 remark as follows: When our Lord went up on high, He left His representative behind Him. This was Holy Church, His mystical Body and Bride, a Divine Institution, and the shrine and organ of the Paraclete, who speaks through her till the end comes. She, to use an Anglican poet's words, is "His very self below" as far as men on earth are equal to the discharge and fulfillment of high offices, which primarily and supremely are His.

These offices, which specially belong to Him as Mediator, are commonly considered to be three; He is Prophet, Priest, and King; and after His pattern, and in human measure, Holy Church has a triple office too; not the Prophetical alone and in isolation, as these Lectures virtually teach, but three offices, which are indivisible, though diverse, viz. teaching, rule, and sacred ministry. This then is the point on which I shall now insist, the very title of the Lectures I am to criticize suggesting to me how best to criticize them.

I will but say in passing, that I must not in this argument be supposed to forget that the Pope, as the Vicar of Christ, inherits these offices and acts for the Church in them. This is another matter; I am speaking here of the Body of Christ, and the sovereign Pontiff would not be the visible head of that Body, did he not first belong to it. He is not himself the Body of Christ, but the chief part of the Body; I shall have quite opportunities enough in what is to come to show that I duly bear him in mind.

Christianity, then, is at once a philosophy, a political power, and a religious rite: as a religion, it is Holy; as a philosophy, it is Apostolic; as a political power, it is imperial, that is, One and Catholic. As a religion, its special center of action is pastor and flock; as a philosophy, the Schools, as a rule, the Papacy and its Curia.

Though it has exercised these three functions in substance from the first, they were developed in their full proportions one after another, in a succession of centuries; first, in the primitive time it was recognized as a worship, springing up and spreading in the lower ranks of society, and among the ignorant and dependent, and making its power felt by the heroism of its Martyrs and confessors. Then it seized upon the intellectual and cultivated class, and created a theology and schools of learning. Lastly it seated itself, as an ecclesiastical polity, among princes, and chose Rome for its center.

Truth is the guiding principle of theology and theological inquires; devotion and edification, of worship; and of government, expedience. The instrument of theology is reasoning; of worship, our emotional nature; of rule, command and coercion. Further, in man as he is, reasoning tends to rationalism; devotion to superstition and enthusiasm; and power to ambition and tyranny.

Arduous as are the duties involved in these three offices, to discharge one by one, much more arduous are they to administer, when taken in combination. Each of the three has its separate scope and direction; each has its own interests to promote and further; each has to find room for the claims of the other two; and each will find its own line of action influenced and modified by the others, nay, sometimes in a particular case the necessity of the others converted into a rule of duty for itself.

5

"Who," in St. Paul's words, "is sufficient for these things?" Who, even with divine aid, shall successfully administer offices so independent of each other, so divergent, and so conflicting? What line of conduct, except on the long, the very long run, is at once edifying, expedient, and true? Is it not plain, that, if one determinate course is to be taken by the Church, acting at once in all three capacities, so opposed to each other in their idea, that course must, as I have said, be deflected from the line which would be traced out by any one of them, if viewed by itself, or else the requirements of one or two sacrificed to the interests of the third? What, for instance, is to be done in a case when to enforce a theological point, as the Schools determine it, would make a particular population less religious, not more so, or cause riots or risings? Or when to defend a champion of ecclesiastical liberty in one country would encourage an anti-Pope, or hazard a general persecution, in another? Or when either a schism is to be encountered or an opportune truth left undefined?

All this was foreseen certainly by the Divine Mind, when He committed to His Church so complex a mission; and, by promising her infallibility in her formal teaching, He indirectly protected her from serious error in worship and political action also. This aid, however, great as it is, does not secure her from all dangers as regards the problem which she has to solve; nothing but the gift of impeccability granted to her authorities would secure them from all liability to mistake in their conduct, policy, words and decisions, in her legislative and her executive, in ecclesiastical and disciplinarian details; and such a gift they have not received. In consequence, however well she may perform her duties on the whole, it will always be easy for her enemies to make a case against her, well founded or not, from the action or interaction, or the chronic collisions or contrasts, or the temporary suspense or delay, of her administration, in her three several departments of duty – her government, her devotions, and her schools – from the conduct of her rulers, her divines, her pastors, or her people.

It is this difficulty lying in the nature of the case, which supplies the staple of those energetic charges and vivid pictures of the inconsistency, double-dealing, and deceit of the Church of Rome, as found in Protestant writings, and in particular in the Lectures and other publications here immediately under consideration.

6

For instance, the Author says in Lecture iii.: "There are two elements in operation within the Roman system. As far as it is Catholic and scriptural, it appeals to the Fathers; as far as it is a corruption, it finds it necessary to supersede them. Viewed in its formal principles and authoritative statements, it professes to be the champion of past times; viewed as an active and political power, as a ruling, grasping, ambitious principle, in a word, as what is expressively called Popery, it exalts the will and pleasure of the existing Church above all authority, whether of Scripture or Antiquity, interpreting the one and disposing of the other by its absolute and arbitrary decree."

That is, the Regal function of the Church, as represented by the Pope, seems to be trampling on the theological, as represented by Scripture and Antiquity.

Again, in Lecture i.: "Members of our Church, in controversy with Rome, contend that it must be judged, not by the formal decrees of the Council of Trent, but by its practical working and existing state in the countries which profess it. Romanists would fain confine us in controversy to a consideration of the bare and acknowledged principles of their Church; we consider it to be an unfair restriction; why? Because we conceive that Romanism is far more faulty in its details than in its formal principles.

That is, the Church, as a political and popular power, is answerable in her past and present history for innumerable acts which go far beyond any theological definitions in the Council of Trent.

Again in Tract 71: – "They claim to be judged by their formal documents, especially by the decrees of the Council of Trent; but, though the acts of individuals are not the acts of the Church, yet they may be the results, and therefore illustrations of its principles. We cannot consent then to confine ourselves to the text of the Tridentine Decrees apart from the teaching of their doctors and the practice of the Church. It is not unnatural to take their general opinions and conduct in elucidation of their synodal decrees."

That is, the current history and ordinary ways of Catholicity, as sanctioned by its rulers and instanced individually in its people, scandalous as they are, must be after all the logical result of the innocent-looking Tridentine decrees.

And to Dr. Jelf: "The doctrine of the schools is at present, on the whole, the established creed of the Roman Church, and this I call Popery, and against this I think the Thirty-Nine Articles speak. I think they speak, not of certain accidental practices, but of a body and substance of divinity, and that traditionary – of an existing, ruling spirit and view in the Church, which, whereas it is a corruption and perversion of the truth, is also a very active and energetic principle, and, whatever holier manifestations there may be in the same Church, manifests itself in ambition, insincerity, craft, cruelty, and all such other grave evils as are connected with these. Further, I believe that the Decrees of Trent, though not necessarily in themselves tending to the corruptions which we see, will ever tend to foster and produce them; that is, while these decrees remain unexplained in any truer and more Catholic way."

That is, there may indeed be holiness in the religious aspect of the Church, and soundness in her theological, but still there is in her the ambition, craft, and cruelty of a political power.

7

I am to apply then the doctrine of the triple office of the Church in explanation of this phenomenon, which gives so much offense to Protestants; and I begin by admitting the general truth of the facts alleged against us; at the same time in the passages just quoted there is one misconception of fact which needs to be corrected before I proceed. The Author of them ascribes the corruptions and other scandals, which he laments in the action of the Church, to the Schools; but ambition, craft, cruelty, and superstition are not commonly the characteristic of theologians, and the natural and proper function of the Schools lies and has lain in forming those abstract decrees which the Author considers to be the least blamable portion of Roman teaching. Nor, again, is it even accurate to say, as he does, that those so-called corruptions are at least the result and development of those abstract decrees: on the contrary, they bear on their face the marks of having a popular or a political origin, and in fact theology, so far from encouraging them, has restrained and corrected such extravagances as have been committed, through human infirmity, in the exercise of the regal and sacerdotal powers; nor is religion ever in greater danger than when, in consequence of national or international troubles, the Schools of theology have been broken up and ceased to be.

And this will serve as a proposition with which to begin. I say, then, Theology is the fundamental and regulating principle of the whole Church system. It is commensurate with Revelation, and Revelation is the initial and essential idea of Christianity. It is the subject-matter, the formal cause, the expression, of the Prophetical Office, and, as being such, has created both the Regal Office and the Sacerdotal. And it has in a certain sense a power of jurisdiction over those offices, as being its own creations, theologians being ever in request and in employment in keeping within bounds both the political and popular elements in the Church's constitution, elements which are far more congenial than itself to the human mind, are far more liable to excess and corruption, and are ever struggling to liberate themselves from those restraints which are in truth necessary for their well-being. On the one hand Popes, such as Liberius,Vigilius, Boniface VIII., and Sixtus V., under secular inducements of the moment, seem from time to time to have been wishing, though unsuccessfully, to venture beyond the lines of theology; and on the other hand, private men of an intemperate devotion are from time to time forming associations, or predicting events, or imagining miracles, so unadvisedly as to call for the interference of the Index or Holy Office. It is not long since the present Pope in his exercise of the Prophetical Office, warned the faithful against putting trust in certain idle prophecies which were in circulation, disallowed a profession of miracles, and forbade some new and extravagant titles which had been given to the Blessed Virgin.

8

Yet theology cannot always have its own way; it is too hard, too intellectual, too exact, to be always equitable, or to be always compassionate; and it sometimes has a conflict or overthrow, or has to consent to a truce or a compromise, in consequence of the rival force of religious sentiment or ecclesiastical interests; and that, sometimes in great matters, sometimes in unimportant.

As a familiar illustration of the contrast with each other which the theological and the religious elements present in their bearing towards the same subject, I am led to notice some words of a Protestant writer incidentally quoted *infr.* p. 66. Theology lays down the undeniable truth (as derived from such passages as "God is not *unjust* to forget your work," &c. Heb. vi. 10) that our good works have merit and are a ground of confidence for us in God's judgment of us. This dogma shocks good Protestants, who think that, in the case of an individual Catholic, it is the mark of a self-righteous spirit, and incompatible with his renunciation of his own desert and with a recourse to God's mercy. But they confuse an intellectual view with a personal sentiment. Now it is well known that Bellarmine has written on Justification, and of course in his treatise he insists, as a theologian must, on the doctrine of merit; but it also happens he is led on, as if he was praying or preaching or giving absolution, to drop some few words, beyond the limits of his science, about his own or his brethren's unworthiness and need of pardon and grace. That is, he has happened to let his devout nature betray itself between the joints of his theological harness. He says, "On account of the uncertainty of our own righteousness and the danger of vain-glory, *it is safest* to place our *whole* trust in the *sole* mercy and goodness of God." What Bellarmine says every theologian *in propriâ personâ* will say; nevertheless the doctrine of merit is a great truth. However, Mr. Bickersteth thinks his confession wonderful, and, as a charitable man, rejoices in it. He looks on him as "a brand from the burning." "I cannot read," he says, "the pious practical works of Bellarmine, himself the great defender of Popery, and know that he said 'Upon account of the uncertainty of life it is most safe to rely on Christ alone,' without hoping that he was led before his death to renounce all confidence in anything but God's testimony concerning His Son, and so became a child of our heavenly Father, and an heir of our Saviour's kingdom."

Again, I have already referred to the dilemma which has occurred before now in the history of the Church, when a choice had to be made between leaving a point of faith at a certain moment undefined, and indirectly opening the way to some extended and permanent schism. Here her Prophetical function is impeded for a while in its action, perhaps seriously, by the remonstrances of charity and of the spirit of peace.

In another familiar instance which may be given, the popular and scholastic elements in the Church seem to change parts, and theology to be kind and sympathetic and religion severe. I mean, whereas the whole School with one voice speaks of freedom of conscience as a personal prerogative of each individual, on the other hand the vow of obedience may sometimes in particular cases be enforced by Religious Superiors in some lesser matter to the conceivable injury of such sacred freedom of thought.

Another instance of collision in a small matter is before us just at this time, the theological and religious element of the Church being in antagonism with the political. Humanity, a sense of morality, hatred of a special misbelief, views of Scripture prophecy, a feeling of brotherhood with Russians, Greeks, and Bulgarians, though schismatics, have determined some of us against the Turkish cause; and a dread lest Russia, if successful, should prove a worse enemy to the Church than Turks can be, determines others of us in favour of it.

9

But I will come to illustrations which involve more difficult questions. Truth is the principle on which all intellectual, and therefore all theological inquiries proceed, and is the motive power which gives them effect; but the principle of popular edification, quickened by a keen sensitiveness of the chance of scandals, is as powerful as Truth, when the province is Religion. To the devotional mind what is new and strange is as repulsive, often as dangerous, as falsehood is to the scientific. Novelty is often error to those who are unprepared for it, from the refraction with which it enters into their conceptions. Hence popular ideas on religion are practically a match for the clearest *dicta,* deductions, and provisos of the Schools, and will have their way in cases when the particular truth, which is the subject of them, is not of vital or primary importance. Thus, in a religion, which embraces large and separate classes of adherents, there always is of necessity to a certain extent an exoteric and an esoteric doctrine.

The history of the Latin versions of the Scriptures furnishes a familiar illustration of this conflict between popular and educated faith. The Gallican version of the Psalter, St. Jerome's earlier work, got such possession of the West, that to this day we use it instead of his later and more correct version from the Hebrew. Devotional use prevailed over scholastic accuracy in a matter of secondary concern. "Jerome," says Dr. Westcott,[2] "was accused of disturbing the repose of the Church, and shaking the foundations of faith;" and perhaps there was good reason for alarm. In the event "long use made it impossible to substitute his Psalter from the Hebrew," and the Gallican version, unless I mistake, is the text of our present Psalter.[3] A parallel anxiety for the same reason is felt at this time within the Anglican communion, upon the proposal to amend King James's Translation of the Scriptures.

10

Here we see the necessary contrast between religious inquiry or teaching, and investigation in purely secular matters. Much is said in this day by men of science about the duty of honesty in what is called the pursuit of truth – by "pursuing truth" being meant the pursuit of facts. It is just now reckoned a great moral virtue to be fearless and thorough in inquiry into facts; and, when science crosses and breaks the received path of Revelation, it is reckoned a serious imputation upon the ethical character of religious men, whenever they show hesitation to shift at a minute's warning their position, and to accept as truths shadowy views at variance with what they have ever been taught and have held. But the contrast between the cases is plain. The love and pursuit of truth in the subject-matter of religion, if it be genuine, must always be accompanied by the fear of error, of error which may be sin. An inquirer in the province of religion is under a responsibility for his reasons and for their issue. But, whatever be the real merits, nay, virtues, of inquirers into physical or historical facts, whatever their skill, their acquired caution, their experience, their dispassionateness and fairness of mind, they do not avail themselves of these excellent instruments of inquiry as a matter of conscience, but because it is expedient, or honest, or beseeming, or praiseworthy, to use them; nor, if in the event they were found to be wrong as to their supposed discoveries, would they, or need they, feel aught of the remorse and self-reproach of a Catholic, on whom it breaks that he has been violently handling the text of Scripture, misinterpreting it, or superseding it, on an hypothesis which he took to be true, but which turns out to be untenable.

Let us suppose in his defense that he was challenged either to admit or to refute what was asserted, and to do so without delay; still it would have been far better could he have waited awhile, as the event has shown – nay, far better, even though the assertion has proved true. Galileo might be right in his conclusion that the earth moves; to consider him a heretic might have been wrong; but there was nothing wrong in censuring abrupt, startling, unsettling, unverified disclosures, if such they were, disclosures at once uncalled for and inopportune, at a time when the limits of revealed truth had not as yet been ascertained. A man ought to be very sure of what he is saying, before he risks the chance of contradicting the word of God. It was safe, not dishonest, to be slow in accepting what nevertheless turned out to be true. Here is an instance in which the Church obliges Scripture expositors, at a given time or place, to be tender of the popular religious sense.

11

I have been led on to take a second view of this matter. That jealousy of originality in the matter of religion, which is the instinct of piety, is, in the case of questions which excite the popular mind, the dictate of charity also. Galileo's truth is said to have shocked and scared the Italy of his day. It revolutionized the received system of belief as regards heaven, purgatory, and hell, to say that the earth went round the sun, and it forcibly imposed upon categorical statements of Scripture, a figurative interpretation. Heaven was no longer above, and earth below; the heavens no longer opened and shut; purgatory and hell were not for certain under the earth. The catalogue of theological truths was seriously curtailed. Whither did our Lord go on His ascension? If there is to be a plurality of worlds, what is the special importance of this one? And, is the whole visible universe with its infinite spaces, one day to pass away? We are used to these questions now, and reconciled to them; and on that account are no fit judges of the disorder and dismay, which the Galilean hypothesis would cause to good Catholics, as far as they became cognizant of it, or how necessary it was in charity, especially then, to delay the formal reception of a new interpretation of Scripture, till their imaginations should gradually get accustomed to it.

12

As to the particular measures taken at the time with this end, I neither know them accurately, nor have I any anxiety to know them. They do not fall within the scope of my argument; I am only concerned with the principle on which they were conducted. All I say is, that not all knowledge is suited to all minds; a proposition may be ever so true, yet at a particular time and place may be "temerarious, offensive to pious ears, and scandalous," though not "heretical" nor "erroneous." It must be recollected what very strong warnings we have from our Lord and St. Paul against scandalizing the weak and unintellectual. The latter goes into detail upon the point. He says, that, true as it may be that certain meats are allowable, this allowance cannot in charity be used in a case in which it would be of spiritual injury to others. "Take care," he says, "that you put not a stumbling-block or a scandal in your brother's way;" "destroy not the work of God for meat;" "it is good to abstain from everything whereby thy brother is offended, or scandalized, or made weak; there is not knowledge in every one," but "take heed lest your liberty become a stumbling-block to the weak." "All things are lawful to me, but not all edify; do not eat for his sake who spoke of it, and for conscience sake, conscience, not thine own, but the other's."[4]

Now, while saying this, I know well that "all things have their season," and that there is not only "a time to keep silence," but "a time to speak," and that, in some states of society, such as our own, it is the worst charity, and the most provoking, irritating rule of action, and the most unhappy policy, not to speak out, not to suffer to be spoken out, all that there is to say. Such speaking out is under such circumstances the triumph of religion, whereas concealment, accommodation, and evasion is to co-operate with the spirit of error – but it is not always so. There are times and places, on the contrary, when it is the duty of a teacher, when asked, to answer frankly as well as truly, though not even then to say more than he need, because learners will but misunderstand him if he attempts more, and therefore it is wiser and kinder to let well alone, than to attempt what is better. I do not say that this is a pleasant rule of conduct, and that it would not be a relief to most men to be rid of its necessity – and for this reason, if for no other, because it is so difficult to apply it aright, so that St. Paul's precept may be interpreted in a particular case as the warrant for just contrary courses of action – but still, it can hardly be denied that there is a great principle in what he says, and a great duty in consequence.

13

In truth we recognize the duty of concealment, or what may be called evasion, not in religious matters only, but universally. It is very well for sublime sciences, which work out their problems apart from the crowding and jostling, the elbowing and the toe-treading of actual life, to care for nobody and nothing but themselves, and to preach and practice the cheap virtue of devotion to what they call truth, meaning of course facts; but a liberty to blurt out all things whatever without self-restraint is not only forbidden by the Church, but by Society at large; of which such liberty, if fully carried out, would certainly be the dissolution. Veracity, like other virtues, lies in a mean. Truth indeed, but not necessarily the whole truth, is the rule of Society. Every class and profession has its secrets; the family lawyer, the medical adviser, the politician, as well as the priest. The physician often dares not tell the whole truth to his patient about his case, knowing that to do so would destroy his chance of recovery. Statesmen in Parliament, I suppose, fight each other with second-best arguments, the real reasons for the policy which they are respectively advocating being, as each is conscious to each, not these, but reasons of state, secrets whether of her Majesty's Privy Council or of diplomacy. As to the polite world, which, to be sure, is in itself not much of an authority, I think an authoress of the last century illustrates in a tale how it would not hold together, if every one told the whole truth to every one, as to what he thought of him. From the time that the Creator clothed Adam, concealment is in some sense the necessity of our fall.

14

This, then, is one cause of that twofold or threefold aspect of the Catholic Church, which I have set myself to explain. Many popular beliefs and practices have, in spite of theology, been suffered by Catholic prelates, lest, "in gathering up the weeds," they should "root up the wheat with them." We see the operation of this necessary economy in the instance of the Old Covenant, in the gradual disclosures made, age after age, to the chosen people. The most striking of these accommodations is the long sufferance of polygamy, concubinage, and divorce. As to divorce, our Lord expressly says to the Pharisees, that "Moses, by reason of the hardness of their hearts, permitted them to put away their wives;" yet this was a breach of a natural and primeval law, which was in force at the beginning as directly and unequivocally as the law against fratricide. St. Augustine seems to go further still, as if not only a tacit toleration of an imperfect morality was observed towards Israel by his Divine Governor, but positive commands were issued in accordance with that state of imperfection in which the people lay. "Only the True and Good God," he says in answer to the Manichee objecting to him certain of the Divine acts recorded in the Old Testament, "only He knows what commands are to be given to individual men. He had given the command, who certainly knows . . . according to the heart of each, what and by means of whom each individual ought to suffer. They deserved, then, the one party to be told to inflict suffering, the other to have to bear it."[5]

This indeed is the great principle of Economy, as advocated in the Alexandrian school,[6] which is in various ways sanctioned in Scripture. In some fundamental points indeed, in the Unity and Omnipotence of God, the Mosaic Law, so tolerant of barbaric cruelty, allowed of no condescension to the ethical state of the times; indeed the very end of the Dispensation was to denounce idolatry, and the sword was its instrument of denunciation; but where the mission of the chosen people was not directly concerned, and amid the heathen populations, even idolatry itself was suffered with something of a Divine sanction, as if a deeper sentiment might lie hid under it. Thus Joseph in the time of the Patriarchs had a divining cup and married the daughter of the Priest of Heliopolis. Jonah in a later time was sent to preach penance to the people of Nineveh, but without giving them a hint, or being understood by them to say, that they must abandon their idols; while the sailors, among whom the Prophet had previously been thrown, though idolaters, recognized with great devotion and religious fear the Lord God of heaven and earth. Again, when Balaam had built his seven altars and offered his sacrifices, and prepared his divinations, it is significantly said, that "the Lord *met* him, and put a word in his mouth," yet without any rebuke of his idolatry and magic. And when Naaman asked forgiveness of God if he "bowed down in the temple of Remmon," the Prophet said no more than "Go in peace." And St. Paul tells both the rude and the cultivated idolaters of Lystra and Athens, that God, in times past, while He gave all nations proofs of His Providence, " suffered them to walk in their own ways," and "winked at the times of their ignorance."

15

From the time that the Apostles preached, such toleration in in primary matters of faith and morals is at an end as regards Christendom. Idolatry is a sin against light; and, while it would involve heinous guilt, or rather is impossible, in a Catholic, it is equally inconceivable in even the most ignorant sectary who claims the Christian name; nevertheless, the principle and the use of the Economy has a place, and is a duty still among Catholics, though not as regards the first elements of Revelation. We have still, as Catholics to be forbearing and to be silent in many cases, amid the mistakes, excesses, and superstitions of individuals and of classes of our brethren, which we come across. Also in the case of those who are not Catholic, we feel it a duty sometimes to observe the rule of silence, even when so serious a truth as the *"Extra Ecclesiam nulla salus"*

comes into consideration. This truth, indeed, must ever
be upheld, but who will venture to blame us, or reproach
us with double-dealing, for holding it to be our duty,
though we thus believe, still, in a case when a Protestant,
near death and to all appearance in good faith, is sure,
humanly speaking, not to accept Catholic truth, if urged
upon him, to leave such a one to his imperfect Christianity, and to the mercy of God, and to assist his devotions
as far as he will let us carry him, rather than to precipitate
him at such a moment into controversy which may ruffle
his mind, dissipate his thoughts, unsettle such measure of
faith as he has, and rouse his slumbering prejudices and
antipathies against the Church? Yet this might be represented as countenancing a double aspect of Catholic
doctrine and as evasive and shuffling, theory saying one
thing, and practice sanctioning another.

16

I shelter what I go on to say of the Church's conduct
occasionally towards her own children, under this rule of
her dealing with strangers: The rule is the same in its
principle as that of Moses or St. Paul, or the Alexandrians,
or St. Augustine, though it is applied to other subject-
matters. Doubtless, her abstract standard of religion and
morals in the Schools is higher than that which we witness
in her children in particular countries or at particular
times; but doubtless also, she, like the old prophets before
her, from no fault of hers, is not able to enforce it. Human
nature is in all ages one and the same: as it showed itself
in the Israelites, so it shows itself in the world at large now,
though one country may be better than another. At least,
in some countries, truth and error in religion may be so
intimately connected as not to admit of separation. I have
already referred to our Lord's parable of the wheat and

the cockle. For instance, take the instance of relics; modern divines and historians may have proved that certain recognized relics, though the remains of some holy man, still do not certainly belong to the Saint to whom they are popularly appropriated; and in spite of this, a bishop may have sanctioned a public veneration of them, which has arisen out of this unfounded belief. And so again, without pledging himself to the truth of the legend of a miracle attached to a certain crucifix or picture, he may have viewed with tolerance, nay, with satisfaction, the overflowing popular devotion towards our Lord or the Blessed Virgin, of which that legend is the occasion. He is not sure it is true, and he does not guarantee its truth; he does but approve and praise the devotional enthusiasm of the people, which the legendary fact has awakened. Did indeed their faith and devotion towards Christ rise simply out of that legend, if they made Him their God because something was said to have taken place which had not taken place, then no honest man, who was simply aware of this, could take any part in the anniversary outburst of rejoicing; but he knows that miracles are wrought in the Church in every age, and, if he is far from certain that this was a miracle, he is not certain that it was not; and his case would be somewhat like French ecclesiastics in the beginning of the century, if Napoleon ordered a *Te Deum* for his victory at Trafalgar, they might have shrewd suspicions about the fact, but they would not see their way not to take part in a national festival. Such may be the feeling under which the Church takes part in popular religious manifestations without subjecting them to theological and historical criticism; she is in a choice of difficulties; did she act otherwise, she would be rooting up the wheat with the intruding weeds; she would be "quenching the smoking flax," and endangering the faith and loyalty of a city or a district, for the sake of an intellectual precision which was quite out of place and was not asked of her.

The difficulty of course is to determine the point at which such religious manifestations become immoderate, and an allowance of them wrong; it would be well, if all suspicious facts could be got rid of altogether. Their tolerance may sometimes lead to pious frauds, which are simply wicked. An ecclesiastical superior certainly cannot sanction alleged miracles or prophecies which he knows to be false, or by his silence connive at a tradition of them being started among his people. Nor can he be dispensed of the duty, when he comes into an inheritance of error or superstition, which is immemorial, of doing what he can to alleviate and dissipate it, though to do this without injury to what is true and good, can after all be only a gradual work. Errors of fact may do no harm, and their removal may do much.

17

As neither the local rulers nor the pastors of the Church are impeccable in act nor infallible in judgment, I am not obliged to maintain that all ecclesiastical measures and permissions have ever been praiseworthy and safe precedents. But as to the mere countenancing of superstitions, it must not be forgotten, that our Lord Himself, on one occasion, passed over the superstitious act of a woman who was in great trouble, for the merit of the faith which was the real element in it. She was under the influence of what would be called, were she alive now, a "corrupt" religion, yet she was rewarded by a miracle. She came behind our Lord and touched Him, hoping "virtue would go out of Him," without His knowing it. She paid a sort of fetish reverence to the hem of His garment; she stole, as she considered, something from Him, and was much disconcerted at being found out. When our Lord asked who had touched Him, "fearing and trembling," says St.

Mark, "knowing what was done in her, she came and fell down before Him, and told Him all the truth," as if there were anything to tell to the All-knowing. What was our Lord's judgment on her? "Daughter, thy faith hath made thee whole; go in peace." Men talk of our double aspect now; has not the first age a double aspect? Do not such incidents in the Gospel as this, and the miracle on the swine, the pool of Bethesda, the restoration of the servant's ear, the changing water into wine, the coin in the fish's mouth, and the like, form an aspect of Apostolic Christianity very different from that presented by St. Paul's Pastoral Epistles and the Epistle General of St. John? Need men wait for the Medieval Church in order to make their complaint that the theology of Christianity does not accord with its religious manifestations?

18

This woman, who is so prominently brought before us by three evangelists, doubtless understood that, if the garment had virtue, this arose from its being Christ's; and so a poor Neapolitan crone, who chatters to the crucifix, refers that crucifix in her deep mental consciousness to an original who once hung upon a cross in flesh and blood; but if, nevertheless she is puzzle-headed enough to assign virtue to it in itself, she does no more than the woman in the Gospel, who preferred to rely for a cure on a bit of cloth, which was our Lord's, to directly and honestly addressing Him. Yet He praised her before the multitude, praised her for what might, not without reason, be called an idolatrous act; for in His new law He was opening the meaning of the word "idolatry," and applying it to various sins, to the adoration paid to rich men, to the thirst after gain, to ambition, and the pride of life, idolatries worse in His judgment than the idolatry of igno-

rance, but not commonly startling or shocking to educated minds. And may I not add that this aspect of our
Lord's teaching is quite in keeping with the general drift
of His discourses? Again and again He insists on the
necessity of faith; but where does He insist on the danger
of superstition, an infirmity, which, taking human nature
as it is, is the sure companion of faith, when vivid and
earnest? Taking human nature as it is, we may surely
concede a little superstition, as not the worst of evils, if it
be the price of making sure of faith. Of course it need not
be the price; and the Church, in her teaching function,
will ever be vigilant against the inroad of what is a degra-
dation both of faith and of reason: but considering, as
Anglicans will allow, how intimately the sacramental system is connected with Christianity, and how feeble and
confused is at present the ethical intelligence of the world
at large, it is a distant day, at which the Church will find
it easy, in her oversight of her populations, to make her
Sacerdotal office keep step with her Prophetical. Just now
I should be disposed to doubt whether that nation really
had the faith, which is free in all its ranks and classes from
all kinds and degrees of what is commonly considered
superstition.

19

Worship, indeed, being the act of our devotional nature,
strives hard to emancipate itself from theological restraints. Theology did not create it, but found it in our
hearts, and used it. And it has many shapes and many
objects, and, moreover, these are not altogether unlawful,
though they be many. Undoubtedly the first and most
necessary of all religious truths is the Being, Unity, and
Omnipotence of God, and it was the primary purpose and
work of Revelation to enforce this. But did not that first

truth involve in itself and suggest to the mind with a sympathetic response a second truth, namely, the existence of other beings besides the Supreme? And that for the very reason that He was Unity and Perfection – I mean, a whole world, though to us unknown – in order to people the vast gulf which separates Him from man? And, when our Lord came and united the Infinite and Finite, was it not natural to think, even before Revelation spoke out, that He came to be "the First born of many brethren," all crowned after His pattern with glory and honor? As there is an instinctive course of reasoning which leads the mind to acknowledge the Supreme God, so we instinctively believe in the existence of beings short of Him, though at the same time far superior to ourselves, beings unseen by us, and yet about us and with relations to us. And He has by His successive revelations confirmed to us the correctness of our anticipation. He has in fact told of the myriads of beings, good and evil, spirits as God is, friendly or hostile to us, who are round about us; and, moreover, by teaching us also the immortality of man, He sets before us a throng of innumerable souls, once men, who are dead neither to God nor to us, and, who, as having been akin to us, suggest to us, when we think of them, and seem to sanction, acts of mutual intercourse.

20

Revelation in this matter does but complete what Nature has begun. It is difficult to deny that polytheism is a natural sentiment corrupted. Its radical evil is, not the belief in many divine intelligences, but its forgetfulness of their Creator, the One Living Personal God who is above them all – that is, its virtual Atheism. First secure in the mind and heart of individuals, in the popular intelligence, a lively faith and trust in Him, and then the *cultus* of Angels and Saints, though ever to be watched with jealousy by theologians, because of human infirmity and perverseness, is a privilege, nay a duty, and has a normal place in revealed Religion.

Holding then this recognition of orders of beings between the Supreme Creator and man to a natural and true sentiment, I have a difficulty in receiving the opinion of the day that monotheism and polytheism are the characteristics of distinct races, the former of the Semitic, the latter of the Aryan. I cannot indeed see the justice of this contrast at all. Did not the Israelites, for all their Semitic descent, worship Baal and Astoreth in the times of the Judges, and sacrifice to these and other false gods under their Kings? And then, when at last a sense of the Divine Unity had been wrought into them, did they not still pay religious honours to Abraham, up to teaching, as our Lord's language shows, that his bosom was the limbo of holy souls? And did not our Lord sanction them in doing so? And this in spite of the danger of superstition in such beliefs, as shown afterwards in St. Paul's warning against Angel worship in his Epistle to the Colossians.

Again, the Saracenic race is Semitic, yet the Arabian Nights suffice to show how congenial the idea of beings intermediate to God and man was to that and other Mohammedan people. In spite of the profession of their religion to uphold severely the Divine Unity, they are notorious for superstitions founded on the belief of innumerable spirits in earth and heaven. Such is their doctrine of Angels, and the stories they attach to them; of whom a large host waits upon every Mussulman, in so much that each of his limbs and functions has its guardian. Such again is that fantastic and fertile mythology, of which Solomon is the central figure; with its population of peris, gins, devis, afreets, and the like, and its bearing upon human affairs. And such again their magic, their charms, spells, lucky and unlucky numbers; and such their belief in astrology. Their insistence on the Divine Unity is rather directed against the Holy Trinity, than against polytheism.

Still more readily will that true theology, which teaches that He ever was a Father in His incomprehensible essence, accept and proclaim the doctrine of the fertility, bountifulness and beneficence of His creative power, and claim for Him the right of a Father over the work of His hands. All things are His and He is in all things. All things are "very good," and, in St. Paul's words, we may "glorify Him in" them. This is especially true as regards intellectual and holy beings, and is the very principle of the *cultus* of Angels and Saints, nor would there be anything to guard against or explain, were it not for the moral sickness and feebleness which is the birth-portion of our race, and which, as the same Apostle affirms, has led them to "change the truth of God into a lie, and worship and serve the creature rather than the Creator, who is blessed for ever."

21

Here at last I come to the point, which has been the drift of these remarks. The primary object of Revelation was to recall men from idolizing the creature. The Israelites had the mission of effecting this by the stern and pitiless ministry of the sword. The Christian Church, after the pattern of our Lord's gentleness, has been guided to an opposite course. Moses on his death was buried by Divine Agency, lest, as the opinion has prevailed, a people, who afterwards offered incense to the brazen serpent which he set up, should be guilty of idolatry towards his dead body. But Christians on the contrary, have from the first cherished and honoured with a special *cultus* the memories of the Martyrs, who had shed their blood for Christ, and have kept up a perpetual communion with all their brethren departed by their prayers and by masses for their souls. That is, the Christian Church has understood that her mission was not like that of Moses, to oppose herself to impulses which were both natural and legitimate though they had been heretofore the instruments of sin, but to do her best, by a right use, to moderate and purify them. Hence, in proportion as the extinction of the old corrupt heathenism made it possible, she has invoked saints, sanctioned the use of their images, and, in the spirit of the Gospels and the Acts, has expected miracles from their persons, garments, relics, and tombs.

This being her mission, not to forbid the memory and veneration of Saints and Angels, but to subordinate it to the worship of the Supreme Creator, it is not wonderful, if she has appeared to lookers-on to be sanctioning and reviving that "old error" which has "passed away;" and that the more so, because she has not been able to do all she could wish against it, and has been obliged at times and in particular cases, as I have said above, as the least of evils, to temporize and compromise – of course short of any infringement of the Revealed Law or any real neglect of her teaching office. And hence, which is our main subject, there will ever be a marked contrariety between the professions of her theology and the ways and doings of a Catholic country.

22

It must be recollected, that, while the Catholic Church is ever most precise in her enunciation of doctrine, and allows no liberty of dissent from her decisions (for on such objective matters she speaks with the authority of infallibility), her tone is different, in the sanction she gives to devotions, as they are of a subjective and personal nature. Here she neither prescribes measure, nor forbids choice, nor, except so far as they imply doctrine, is she infallible in her adoption or use of them. This is an additional reason why the formal decrees of Councils and statements of theologians differ in their first aspect from the religion of the uneducated classes; the latter represents the wayward popular taste, and the former the critical judgments of clear heads and holy hearts.

This contrast will be the greater, when, as sometimes happens, ecclesiastical authority takes part with the popular sentiment against a theological decision. Such, we know, was the case, when St. Peter himself committed an error in conduct, in the countenance he gave to the Mosaic rites in consequence of the pressure exerted on him by the Judaic Christians. On that occasion St. Paul withstood him, "because he was to be blamed." A fault, which even the first Pope incurred, may in some other matter of rite or devotion find a place now and then in the history of holy and learned ecclesiastics who were not Popes. Such an instance seems presented to us in the error of judgment which was committed by the Fathers of the Society of Jesus in China, in their adoption of certain customs which they found among the heathen there; and Protestant writers in consequence have noted it as a signal instance of the double-faced conduct of Catholics, as if they were used to present their religion under various aspects according to the expedience of the place or time. But that there is a religious way of thus accommodating ourselves to those among whom we live, and whom it is our duty, if possible, to convert, is plain from St. Paul's own rule of life considering he "became to the Jews as a Jew, that he might gain the Jews, and to them that were without the law, as if he were without the law, and became all things to all men that he might save all." Or what, shall we say to the commencement of St. John's Gospel, in which the Evangelist may be as plausibly represented to

have used the language of heathen classics with the purpose of interesting and gaining the Platonizing Jews, as
the Jesuits be charged with duplicity and deceit in aiming
at the conversion of the heathen in the East by an imita-
tion of their customs. St. Paul on various occasions acts in
the same spirit of economy, as did the great Missionary
Church of Alexandria in the centuries which followed; its
masters did but carry out, professedly, a principle of
action, of which they considered they found examples in
Scripture. Anglicans who appeal to the ante-Nicene period as especially their own, should be tender of the
memories of Theonas, Clement, Origen, and Gregory
Thaumaturgus.

23

The mention of missions and of St. Gregory leads me on
to another department of my general subject, viz. the
embarrassments and difficult questions arising out of the
regal office of the Church and her duties to it. It is said
of this primitive Father, who was the Apostle of a large
district in Asia Minor, that he found in it only seventeen
Christians, and on his death left in it only seventeen
pagans. This was an enlargement of the Church's territory
worthy of a Catholic Bishop, but how did he achieve it?
Putting aside the real cause, the Divine blessing, and his
gift of miracles, we are told of one special act of his, not
unlike that of the Jesuits in the East, which I will relate in
the words of Neander: "Having observed that many of the
common people were attached to the religion of their
fathers from a love of the ancient sports connected with
paganism, he determined to provide the new converts
with a substitute for those. He instituted a general festival
in honour of the Martyrs, and permitted the rude multi-
tudes to celebrate it with banquets similar to those which

accompanied the pagan funerals (*parentalia*) and other heathen festivals."[7]

Neander indeed finds fault with Gregory's indulgence, and certainly it had its dangers, as all such economies have, and it required anxious vigilance on the part of a Christian teacher in carrying it out. St. Peter Chrysologus, in the fifth century, when Christianity needed no such expedients, expressed this feeling when, on occasion of the heathen dances usual in his diocese on the Calends of January, he said, " Whoso will have his joke with the devil, will not have his triumph with Christ." But, I suppose, both measures at once, the indulgence and the vigilance, were included in St. Gregory's proceeding, as in other times and places in the Church's history. At this very time Carnival is allowed, if not sanctioned, by ecclesiastical authorities in the cities of the Continent, while they not only keep away from it themselves, but appoint special devotions in the Churches, in order to draw away the faithful from the spiritual dangers attending on it.

24

St. Gregory was a Bishop as well as a preacher and spiritual guide, so that the economy which is related of him is an act of the regal function of the Church, as well as of her sacerdotal and pastoral. And this indeed attaches to most of the instances which I have been giving above of the Church's moderating or suspending under circumstances the requisitions of her theology. They illustrate at once both these elements of her divinely ordered constitution; for the fear, as already mentioned, of "quenching the smoking flax," which is the attribute of a guide of souls, operated in the same direction as zeal for the extension of Christ's kingdom, in resisting that rigorousness of a logical theology which is more suited for the Schools than for the world. In these cases then the two offices, political and pastoral, have a common interest as against the theological; but this is not always so, and therefore I shall now go on to give instances in which the imperial and political expedience of religion stands out prominent, and both its theological and devotional duties are in the background.

25

I observe then that Apostolicity of doctrine and Sanctity of worship, as attributes of the Church, are differently circumstanced from her regal autocracy. Tradition in good measure is sufficient for doctrine, and popular custom and conscience for worship, but tradition and custom cannot of themselves secure independence and self-government. The Greek Church shows this, which has lost its political life, while its doctrine, and its ritual and devotional system, have little that can be excepted against. If the Church is to be regal, a witness for Heaven, unchangable amid secular changes, if in every age she is to hold her own, and proclaim as well as profess the truth, if she is to thrive without or against the civil power, if she is to be resourceful and self-recuperative under all fortunes, she must be more than Holy and Apostolic; she must be Catholic. Hence it is that, first, she has ever from her beginning onwards had a hierarchy and a head, with a strict unity of polity, the claim of an exclusive divine authority and blessing, the trusteeship of the gospel gifts, and the exercise over her members of an absolute and almost despotic rule. And next, as to her work, it is her special duty, as a sovereign State, to consolidate her several portions, to enlarge her territory, to keep up and to increase her various populations in this ever-dying, ever-nascent world, in which to be stationary is to lose ground, and to repose is to fail. It is her duty to strengthen and facilitate the intercourse of city with city, and race with race, so that an injury done to one is felt to be an injury to all, and the act of individuals has the energy and momentum of the whole body. It is her duty to have her eyes upon the movements of all classes in her wide dominion, on ecclesiastics and laymen, on the regular clergy and secular, on civil society, and political movements. She must be on the watchtower, discerning in the distance and providing against all dangers; she has to protect the ignorant and weak, to remove scandals, to see to the education of the young, to administer temporalities, to initiate, or at least to direct all Christian work, and all with a view to the life, health, and strength of Christianity, and the salvation of souls.

It is easy to understand how from time to time such serious interests and duties involve, as regards the parties who have the responsibility of them, the risk, perhaps the certainty, at least the imputation, of ambition or other selfish motive, and still more frequently of error in judgment, or violent action, or injustice. However, leaving this portion of the subject with this remark, I shall bring what I have to say to an end by putting the Regal office of the Church side by side with the Prophetical, and giving instances of the collisions and compromises which have taken place between them in consequence of their respective duties and interests.

26

For example: the early tradition of the Church was dissuasive of using force in the maintenance of religion. "It is not the part of men who have confidence in what they believe," says Athanasius, "to force and compel the unwilling. For the truth is not preached with swords, or with darts, nor by means of soldiers, but by persuasion and counsel." *Arian. Hist. § 33.* Augustine at first took the same view of duty; but his experience as Bishop led him to change his mind. Here we see the interests of the Church, as a regal power, acting as an influence upon his theology.

Again: with a view to the Church's greater unity and strength, Popes, from the time of St. Gregory I, down to the present, have been earnest in superseding and putting away the diversified traditional forms of ritual in various parts of the Church. In this policy ecclesiastical expedience has acted in the subject-matter of theology and worship.

Again: acts simply unjustifiable such as real betrayals of the truth on the part of Liberius and Honorius, become intelligible, and cease to be shocking, if we consider that those Popes felt themselves to be head rulers of Christendom and their first duty, as such, to be that of securing its peace, union and consolidation. The personal want of firmness or of clear-sightedness in the matter of doctrine, which each of them in his own day evidenced, may have arisen out of his keen sense of being the Ecumenical Bishop and one Pastor of Christ's flock, of the scandal caused by its internal dissensions, and of his responsibility, should it retrograde in health and strength in his day.

27

The principle, on which these two Popes may be supposed to have acted, not unsound in itself, though by them wrongly applied, I conceive to be this – that no act could be theologically an error, which was absolutely and undeniably necessary for the unity, sanctity, and peace of the Church; for falsehood never could be necessary for those blessings, and truth alone can be. If one could be sure of this necessity, the principle itself may be granted; though, from the difficulty of rightly applying it, it can only be allowed on such grave occasions, with so luminous a tradition, in its favour, and by such high authorities, as make it safe. If it was wrongly used by the Popes whom I have named, it has been rightly and successfully used by others, in whose decision, in their respective cases, no Catholic has any difficulty in concurring.

28

I will give some instances of it, and of these the most obvious is our doctrine regarding the Canonization of Saints. The infallibility of the Church must certainly extend to this solemn and public act; and that, because on so serious a matter, affecting the worship of the faithful, though relating to a fact, the Church (that is, the Pope), must be infallible. This is Cardinal Lambertini's decision, in concurrence with St. Thomas, putting on one side the question of the Pope's ordinary infallibility, which depends on other arguments. *"It cannot be,"* that great author says, "that the Universal Church should be led into error on a point of morals by the supreme Pontiff; and that certainly would, or might happen, supposing he could be mistaken in a canonization." This, too, is St. Thomas's argument: "In the Church there can be no damnable error; but this would be such, if one who was really a sinner, were venerated as a saint," &c. – Card Lambert. *de Canon.* Diss. xxi. vol. 1. ed. Ven. 1751.

29

Again: in like manner, our certainty that the Apostolic succession of Bishops in the Catholic Church has no flaw in it, and that the validity of the Sacraments is secure, in spite of possible mistakes and informalities in the course of 1800 years, rests upon our faith that He who has decreed the end has decreed the means – that He is always sufficient for His Church – that, if He has given us a promise ever to be with us, He will perform it.

30

A more delicate instance of this argument, *ex absurdo,* as it may be called, is found in the learned book of Morinus "de Ordinationibus." He shows us that its application was the turning-point of the decision ultimately made at Rome in the middle age, in regard to simoniacal, heretical, and schismatical ordinations. As regards ordinations made with simony, it seems that Pope Leo IX, on occasion of the ecclesiastical disorders of his time, held a solemn Council, in which judgment was given against the validity of such acts. It seems also that, from certain ecclesiastical difficulties which followed, lying in the region of fact, from the *"incommoda hinc emergentia,"* the Pope could not carry out the Synodal act, and was obliged to issue a milder decision instead of it. St. Peter Damiani, giving an account of this incident, says, "When Leo pronounced all simoniacal ordinations to be null and void, the consequence was a serious tumult and resistance on the part of the multitude of Roman priests, who urged, with the concurrence of the Bishops, that it would lead to the Basilicas being deprived of the sacerdotal offices; moreover, that the Masses would absolutely cease, to the overthrow of the Christian Religion and the dismay of all the faithful everywhere."

Such a mode of resolving a point in theology is intelligible only on the ground laid down above, that a certain quasi-doctrinal conclusion may be in such wise fatal to the constitution, and therefore to the being of the Church as *ipso facto* to stultify the principles from which it is drawn, it being inconceivable that her Lord and Maker intended that the action of any one of her functions should be the destruction of another. In this case, then, He willed that a point of theology should be determined on its expediency relatively to the Church's Catholicity and the edification of her people – by the logic of facts, which at times overrides all positive laws and prerogatives, and reaches in its effective force to the very frontiers of immutable truths in religion, ethics, and theology.

31

This instance, in which the motive-cause of the decision ultimately made is so clearly brought out, is confirmed by the parallel case of heretical ordination. For instance, Pope Innocent, in the fourth century, writing to the Bishops of Macedonia, concedes the validity of heretical orders in a certain case specified, declaring the while, that such a concession ran counter to the tradition of the Roman Church. This concession was made in order to put an end to a great scandal; but "certainly" the Pope says, "it was not so from the first, as there were ancient rules, which, as handed down from the Apostles and Apostolic men, the Roman Church guards and commits to the guardianship of her subjects."

32

Again, as regards schismatical ordination, as of the Donatists: on this occasion, Rome stood firm to her traditional view, and Augustine apparently concurred in it; but the African Bishops on the whole were actuated by their sense of the necessity of taking the opposite line, and were afraid of committing themselves to the principle that heresy or schism nullified ordination. They condemned (with the countenance of Augustine) Donatus alone, the author of the schism, but accepted the rest, orders and all, lest remaining outside the Church, they should be a perpetual thorn in her side. "It was not possible," says Morinus, "for Augustine to come to any other decision considering he saw daily the Donatists with their orders received into the Church." This is another instance of the schools giving way to ecclesiastical expedience, and of the interests of peace and unity being a surer way of arriving at a doctrinal conclusion than methods more directly theological.

33

The considerations which might be urged, in behalf of these irregular ordinations, on the score of expedience, had still greater force when urged in recognition of heretical baptism, which formed the subject of a controversy in the preceding century. Baptism was held to be the entrance to Christianity and its other sacraments, and once a Christian, ever a Christian. It marked and discriminated the soul receiving it from all other souls by a supernatural character, as the owner's name is imprinted on a flock of sheep. Thus heretics far and wide, if baptized, were children of the Church, and they answered to that title so far as they were in fact preachers of the truth of Christ to the heathen; since there is no religious sect without truth in it, and it would be truth which the heathen had to be taught. That exuberant birth of strange rites and doctrines, which suddenly burst into life all round Christianity on its start, is one of the striking evidences of the wondrous force of the Christian idea, and of its subtle penetrating influence, when it first fell upon the ignorant masses: and though many of these sects had little or no claim to administer a real baptism, and in many or most the abounding evil that was in them choked the scanty and feeble good, yet was the Church definitely to reject a baptism simply on the ground of its not being administered by a Catholic? Expedience pointed out the duty of acknowledging it in cases in which our Lord's description of it, when He made it His initiatory rite, had been exactly fulfilled, unless indeed Scripture and Tradition were directly opposed to such a course. To cut off such cautious baptism from the Church was to circumscribe her range of subjects, and to impair her catholicity. It was to sacrifice those, who, though at present blinded by the mist of error, had enough of truth in their religion, however latent, to leave hope of their conversion at some future day. The imperial See of Peter, ever on the watch for the extension of Christ's kingdom, understood this well; and, while its tradition was unfavourable to heretical ordination, it was strong and clear in behalf of the validity of heretical baptism.

Pope Stephen took this side then in a memorable controversy, and maintained it against almost the whole Christian world. It was a signal instance of the triumph under Divine Providence, of a high, generous expediency over a conception of Christian doctrine, which logically indeed seemed unanswerable. One must grant indeed, as I have said, that he based his decision upon Tradition, not on expediency, but why such a Tradition in the first instance begun? The reason of the Tradition has to be explained; and, if Stephen is not to have the credit of the large and wise views which occasioned his conduct, that credit belongs to the Popes who went before him. These he had on his side certainly, but whom had he besides them? The Apostolical Canons say, "Those who are baptized by heretics cannot be believers." The Synods of Iconium and Synnada declare that "those who came from the heretics were to be washed and purified from the filth of their old impure leaven." Clement of Alexandria, that "Wisdom pronounces that strange waters do not belong to her." Firmilian, that "we recognize one only Church of God, and account baptism to belong only to the Holy Church." "It seemed good from the beginning," says St. Basil, "wholly to annul the baptism of heretics." Tertullian says, "We have not the same baptism with heretics; since they have it not rightly; without, they have it not at all."[8] "Then may there be one baptism," says St. Cyprian, "when there is one faith. We and heretics cannot have a common baptism, since we have not the Father, or the Son, or the Holy Ghost in common. Heretics in their baptism are polluted by their profane water." St. Cyril says, "None but heretics are re-baptized, since their former baptism was not baptism." St. Athanasius asks, "Is not the rite administered by the Arians, altogether empty and unprofitable? He that is sprinkled by them is rather polluted than redeemed." Optatus says, "The stained baptism cannot wash a man, the polluted cannot cleanse." "The baptism of traitors," says St. Ambrose, "does not heal, does not cleanse, but defiles."

Expedience is an argument which grows in cogency with the course of years; a hundred and fifty years after St. Stephen, the ecclesiastical conclusion which he had upheld was accepted generally by the School of Theologians, in an adhesion to it on the part of St. Augustine.

34

Lastly, serious as this contrast is between the decision of the Pope and the logic of the above great authors, there was, before and in his time, a change yet greater in the ideas and the tone of the theological schools; a change which may remind us of the language of Cardinal Fisher on a collateral subject, as is to be found below at p. 72. I mean that relaxation of the penitential canons, effected by a succession of Popes, which, much as it altered the Church's discipline and the ordinary course of Christian life, still was strictly conformable to the necessities of her prospective state, as our Lord had described it beforehand. As Christianity spread through the various classes of the Pagan Empire, and penetrated into private families, social circles, and secular callings, and was received with temporary or local toleration, the standard of duty amongst its adherents fell; habits and practices of the world found their way into the fold; and scandals became too common to allow of the offenders being cast off by wholesale.

This, I say, was but the fulfillment of our Lord's prophetic announcement, that the kingdom of heaven should be a net, gathering fish of every kind; and how indeed should it be otherwise, if it was to be Catholic, human nature being what it is? Yet, on the other hand, the Sermon on the Mount, and other discourses of our Lord, assigned a very definite standard of morals, and a very high rule of conduct to His people. Under these circumstances the Holy See and various Bishops took what would be called the laxer side, as being that which charity, as well as expediency suggested, whereas the graver and more strict, as well as the ignorant portion of the Christian community did not understand such a policy, and in consequence there was, in various parts of the world, both among the educated and the uneducated, an indignant rising against this innovation, as it was conceived, of their rulers. Montanus and his sect in the East, represent the feelings of the multitude at Rome, the school of Tertullian, Novatian, and the author of the Elenchus, able and learned men, stood out in behalf of what they considered the Old Theology, terminating their course in the Novatian schism; while the learned Donatist Bishops and the mad Circumcelliones illustrate a like sentiment, and a like temper, in Africa. During a long controversy, the collision of those elements in the Church's constitution, which have formed the subject of this Essay, is variously illustrated. It carries us through the Pontificates of Zephyrinus, Callistus, Cornelius, Stephen, and Dionysius, and so on down to the Episcopate of St. Augustine; and it ends in the universal acceptance of the decision of the Holy See. The resolution of the difficulties of the problem was found in a clearer recognition of the distinction between precepts and counsels, between mortal sins and venial, and between the two forums of the Church, the external and internal; also in the development of the doctrine of Purgatory, and in the contemporary rise of the monastic institution, as exhibited in the history of St. Antony and his disciples.

35

So much on the collision and the adjustment of the Regal or political office of the Church with the Prophetical: that I may not end without an instance of the political in contrast with the Sacerdotal, I will refer to the Labarum of Constantine. The sacred symbol of unresisting suffering, of self-sacrificing love, of life-giving grace, of celestial peace, became in the hands of the first Christian Emperor, with the sanction of the Church, his banner in fierce battle and the pledge of victory for his sword.

36

To conclude: whatever is great refuses to be reduced to human rule, and to be made consistent in its many aspects with itself. Who shall reconcile with each other the various attributes of the Infinite God? And, as He is, such in their several degrees are His works. This living world to which we belong, how self-contradictory it is, when we attempt to measure and master its meaning and scope! And how full of incongruities, that is, of mysteries, in its higher and finer specimens, is the soul of man, viewed in its assemblage of opinions, tastes, habits, powers, aims, and doings! We need not feel surprise then, if Holy Church too, the supernatural creation of God, is an instance of the same law, presenting to us an admirable consistency and unity in word and deed, as her general characteristic but crossed and discredited now and then by apparent anomalies which need, and which claim, at our hands an exercise of faith.

Endnotes

1. "Viewed as an active and political power, as a ruling, grasping, ambitious principle, in a word, as what is expressively called Popery," *&c., infr.* p. 83. "this system I have called, in what I have written, Romanism or Popery, and by Romanists or Papists I mean all its members so far as they are under the power of these principles," *infr.* vol. 2, Letter to Bishop of Oxford.

2. Smith's Dict. of the Bible, vol. 3, pp. 1702-3.

3. "Note that the Vulgate Psalter is not from St. Jerome's translation of the Hebrew . . . For since the Psalms occupy popular memory, from being used daily and sung in the churches, they could not be altered without giving serious offense. Hence the old version is retained in the Vulgate Psalter." *Nat. Alex. Saec.* iv *Diss.* 39. (ed. trans.)

4. Vid. also 1 Cor. iii, 1, 2 and Heb. v. 12-14.

5. Mozley, Lect. on the O.T. xi., p. 270. "God, who certainly knows, had commanded, not according to mere facts, but according to the human heart, what each one should suffer,

and from whom. . . . Hence those who were commanded, and those who suffered, were treated justly. . . . But, he says, it is not to be believed that a good and true God gave such commands. Rather, only a true and good God could rightly give such commands. . . . Only a true and good God knows what, when, to whom, and by whom, he should command or permit something to be done." *Contr. Faust.*, xxii. 71, 72. (ed. trans.)

6. Vid. Arians of the Fourth Century, p. 67.

7. Hist. vol. ii p. 496 (Bohn)

8. *Vid. infr.* p. 170, and Pusey's *Tertullian*, p. 280.